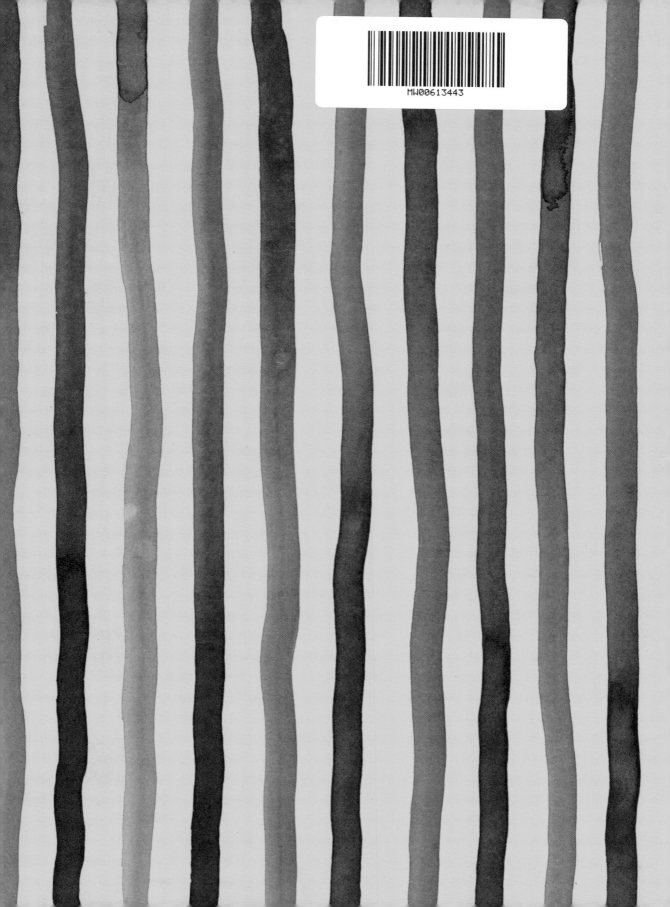

For Saint Lorenzo & Santino
and
for Monica & Mauro

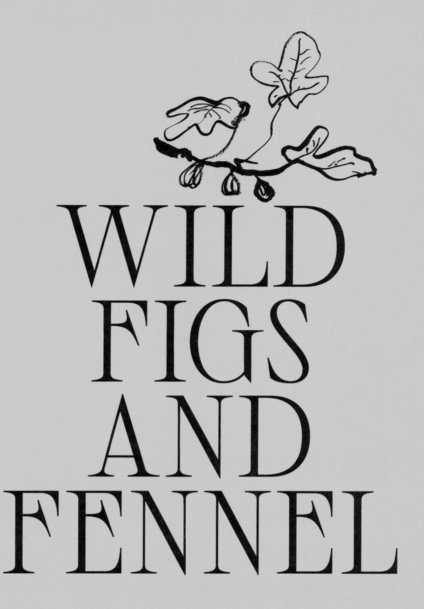

WILD FIGS AND FENNEL

A YEAR IN AN ITALIAN KITCHEN

By LETITIA CLARK

Hardie Grant

BOOKS

CONTENTS

PREFACE

There is something about food in Italy that sticks.

Something that – like a good meal, dish or lover – initially charms, entices and delights, and then slowly satisfies and stays, stuck like a stubborn shred of salami in the teeth.

It is, of course, partly to do with the dishes themselves – a burnished and bubbling lasagne, a glossy plate of pasta, a soft, semola-dusted *panino* stuffed with salty-sweet prosciutto, a shining salad or a perfect peach – but it is more than that, too, because food is always just the beginning.

When I wrote my first book, *Bitter Honey*, I approached an agent with my manuscript, pink and eager as a new-born weasel.

'I'm sorry but it's a no,' he said. 'There are too many Italian recipe books. People have had enough of Italy.'

Deflated, I went home and told Luca what had happened.

'Letizia,' he said. 'Don't talk *fesserie*. People will *never* have enough of Italy. It's like saying people have had enough of love. Or ham.'

'And anyway,' he added after a moment's thought, 'Sardinia is *different*.'

I seem to spend my life trying to define exactly what it is that makes Sardinia different. What I can say, after six years of living here, observing the people, the produce and the place with beady eyes, bothering my Sardinian family and friends with endless questions and reading most of the books I can find, is that Sardinia is a sort of concentrated

version of Italy, a place where many traditional values and customs have been preserved; pickled in time. Most significantly, Sardinia is a place that prioritises those two fundamental pillars of Italian culture and two of the things that matter the most to me: food and family.

This book is dedicated to my family – to both my Sardinian families – the one we are building, and the one I have inherited, all of whom have eaten its contents many times over. Coming together to eat a meal *in famiglia*, whether it is a rushed bowl of *pasta al sugo* or a carefully prepared celebratory feast, is still one of the fundamental joys of everyday life. Sharing food with those you love, bickering and bantering around a table, is something so basic and yet so essential to general wellbeing that we take it for granted, and often do not make the time. The majority of Italians make the time. As Marcella Hazan puts it so well:

'Making time to eat as Italians do is to share in their inexhaustible gift for making art out of life.'

INTRODUCTION

This book charts a year in my Sardinian kitchen. It is a small, unassuming kitchen, with a sink wedged in a dark corner so you can't see if the dishes are dirty or not. In the centre of this kitchen, by the window, is a small, low, rickety table at which we eat our meals; every day, three times a day, with dusty sunbeams shining in our faces or fat raindrops pattering on the fig leaves.

Our lives, as I'm sure yours are too, are governed by the changing seasons. What we eat, what we wear, where we go, what we do. Living in a small town in Sardinia, where a rural way of life is still relatively common, we are forever at the mercy of the wild whims of the weather. For all my life it has been the first thing my family and I do every morning, and the last thing we do every night: *check the weather*. My conversations with my father (and plenty of my friends too) revolve around the respective weather in the UK and Italy: gloating over sunshine, grumbling about rain. The changing seasons, apart from providing an endless source of conversation, give structure to our lives and to our cooking, too.

It has, somewhat sadly, become a cliché to talk about seasonal cooking; a vehicle for inevitable bandwagonism and exclusivity. The true concept of seasonal cooking means one must cook both seasonally and *locally*, because all sorts of things are 'in season' at some point somewhere in the world. Cooking both seasonally and locally is simply the only way of life in Sardinia. Apart from the occasional banana and pineapple (bizarrely especially at Christmas), the majority of the produce available is local, grown less than

a kilometre away. Mauro, my father-in-law, refuses on principle to buy things that have come from Cagliari (a mere 50-minute drive away).

Eating and cooking following these principles can be both limiting and liberating. There are — inevitably — periods of abundance and periods of scarcity. Following the flux of the year, one becomes ever more aware of the innate majesty and magic of nature, and most specifically, of its inherent logic. Each season comes with its own armoury: the feisty citrus to blast away the winter gloom; the electric yellow spritz of lemon just at the cusp of spring; the quenching juice of a scarlet watermelon in August. How can you sit on a hot beach in midsummer, eating an iced slice of melon, or in a cold kitchen in December, eating an orange, and not be filled with awe at these small miracles of natural logic?

This aspect of feast and famine punctuates the Sardinian year. In the winter, we turn to the storecupboard; in the summer, there is so much fruit it provides fodder for the flies. The glut and dearth of primary produce makes a cook creative by default; one must come up with an arsenal of fig recipes in September, and four hundred ways of using artichokes in April. The flow of the seasons, and the produce that comes with them, is the *fil rouge* that underpins our lives. Just as we tire of figs the persimmons come, and so begins another Sardinian autumn. There is a constancy and fluidity to this seasonal way of life that is infinitely reassuring — the ritual, routine and repetition of it, as we live safe in the knowledge that soon it will be June, and there will be cherries again.

SPRING

Primavera

Winds and Wildflowers

The spring is fringed with blossom; beginning with almond and ending with orange. The two trees neatly bookend a season full of flowers. Flowers flock wild on the coastline, climb over crumbling walls and are cultivated in immaculate *ortos* (garden plots). The honey-scented almond blossom is the first to bloom in mid-February, followed by the periwinkle in the hedgerows and the wild honeysuckle that ambles chaotically over the cliffs, clinging to the waxy lentisco. In late April, at the tail-end of the season, the scent of the orange blossom drifts on the evening air, and pale grey doves ruffle their feathers gently, look down on us and coo.

'Describe the Sardinian seasons,' I say to my schoolchildren.

'Sardinia has two seasons, winter and summer,' they reply. 'Spring doesn't exist. It's too cold and then before you know it, it's too hot.'

The official calendar year begins in winter – January the cold frozen heart of winter – but I don't feel alive until the first blossom blooms. By March, the coast is cloaked in lilac, the wild rosemary in flower, stouter and with shorter needles, it has an intensely pungent and saline flavour, and makes the best focaccia of all. Like the tortoises that live wild all over the *macchia mediterranea*, plodding beneath the shrubs of lentisco and helichrysum, we do not stir until spring. And then, after a long, steady climb up the sheer hill to winter, once over the craggy peak at Carnival, we roll, gathering speed and scattering wild flowers, into summer. The tourists arrive in their Volkswagons, fresh and pink, burnt by the treacherous spring sun. The Sardinians, suspicious still, are dressed in four layers of black.

The *primavera* here is more short-lived than those springs I knew in England. Condensed, or concentrated, but not dissimilar. The timid sunshine here, however, even in February, has a sting. I peel and eat a blood orange in a sunbeam and feel the heat on my face. The red juice dries sticky in seconds. I move into the shade, the bees humming sleepily in the blossom.

As March moves to April we become victims once again to the whims of the two winds that blow through the island: the Maestrale and the Scirocco. I come to know these winds as closely as family members. I know their soothing balm and their treacherous natures. The Maestrale, the cooling angel of the North, blowing in from France and bringing fresh, welcome relief; and the devilish Scirocco from the South, hot and heavy and carrying red sand that dirties (scrupulously) cleaned cars. If there is Maestrale we are saved, Scirocco means doom. I've never worried about wind so much in my life. And they say it's the English who are obsessed with the weather.

April can be the cruellest month; breeding blossom sprays of fragile white hope and then battering them with wild winds. We forget ourselves and plan picnics, only to retreat to the car. The ground is a carpet of fallen orange blossom, the bees drunk on nectar, buffeted around by unpredictable breezes, partly pleasurable, partly plain cold; the Botticellian zephyrs of spring. Lorenzo starts eulogising about zephyrs.

'How do you say *zefiro* in English?'

I write this in April, the spring in full swing. In the distance I spy a lone puff of white cloud in an otherwise sapphire sky. An innocent rice krispie floating in a blue so sharp and clear you could reach out and snap off a piece of it.

Lorenzo looks at the tiny, innocent cloud and scowls. He opens the door and sniffs the air, tentatively, like a rabbit.

'A perfect day to get ill,' he says.

He disappears to put on another scarf.

Meanwhile, the olive and the vine begin to break into leaf. The tiny grapes start forming in their clusters, for now just little specks, and the olives are just visible too. It's the time for greens, for foraging, for hedgerows and honey, for ricotta and the first tentative fruit, *nespole* (loquats) and strawberries, still fresh and full of rain. The asphodel is in flower, and my friend Luigi makes the first honey of the year: pale and runny and delicate; a honey for spring.

The hedges and verges are full of wild greens. The wild fennel, which grows all over Sardinia and weaves its characteristic flavour into the wine (Vernaccia specifically) sprouts like a weed, and I pick bunches to keep in a tumbler in the kitchen, and add to soups and salads. It works well in sweets too, specifically in combination with spring fruit. There is wild chard with rhubarb-pink stems, lemony wild sorrel, woody wild asparagus, nettles and wild leeks with their white bell flowers and flat pointed leaves, carpets of them dancing in the wind, reminding me of the bluebell woods we hunted for every spring in England.

A spring shower and the snails are out in droves; the lane dotted with shells striped like humbugs, antlers wheeling and alert, as they make their way, determined, to the other side. What awaits them there who knows, more wild leeks and fennel. Zio Mario will be out picking, the snails now are at their best, he says, fresh and full of fennel, you can taste it in their sweet flesh, which he cooks *al sugo*. They need to be 'purged' first, and though I enjoy the taste and texture when he cooks them, I can't bring myself to undergo this gruesome process, so I pass them politely instead at dawn, weaving my way between them, and wish them well on their way.

The vines are pruned, the land ploughed, the white tablecloths washed and blowing in the breeze. On my evening walks I pick rosy garlic, honey-scented mimosa in scrambled egg pom-poms, more wild leeks and borage.

The strawberries still taste of rain rather than sun-bleached sugar, but a few more days and they will get there. The first *nespole* are cropping, pale orange and pert, their waxy skins easily peeled, their juicy flesh tart and sour-grape-like, infinitely refreshing.

It is a time when I want to start cooking again, and emerge from the soup and sauced-pasta rut; a time to tumble salads and peel and poach vegetables, to prepare endless spiky artichokes, and a time for eggs, the undeniable symbol of spring and rebirth.

Easter crowns the season; a celebration of the peak of citrus, lemons and oranges at their bulging best, and lamb, artichokes and greens for lunch. The whole village gathers in the church.

'*Gesù Cristo Risorto!*' sings the portly priest.

'*Gesù Cristo Risotto!*' squeals a child gleefully in the front row.

We go home and eat risotto with artichokes.

At the end of April I smell the first whiff of hot grass, and I can feel it is coming. Hurrying near, the summer malaise, with its honey-slow heat and peaches. The first fat fly buzzes and butts the window, blue and bulging.

The strawberries in the field I pass every morning are slowly unveiled. They have been shrouded in plastic until now, kept snug. My neighbour visits every morning, tending to them with extraordinary tenderness, cooing and caressing as Kiss' *I Was Made for Lovin' You* plays from his Fiat Punto radio.

Summer is coming.

Lemon Ricotta Soufflé 'Plancakes'

Makes 6 large pancakes (serves 2)

100 g (3½ oz) ricotta (see Note)

1 egg, separated

120 ml (4 fl oz/½ cup) milk

1 tablespoon vanilla sugar
(or plain sugar and a little
vanilla extract)

zest of 1 small lemon

pinch of salt

80 g (3 oz/scant ⅔ cup) plain
(all-purpose) flour

1 teaspoon baking powder

1 tablespoon butter

oil, for greasing

The first time I ever made Lorenzo pancakes he misheard the name and pronounced them 'plan-cakes'. Of course this is now what we call them. I like to make plan-cakes on Sunday mornings while we make plans for the day/week.

These particular plan-cakes are much lighter than the standard offering; they have a delicate, lemony flavour and a wonderfully fluffy, creamy texture. With some macerated berries and yoghurt (or honey) they make the perfect summer breakfast.

I know it may seem like whisking egg whites in the morning is really the last thing you want to do, but it's only one white, you can whisk it by hand (with a fork even) and you'd be amazed how fast it is. I find it strangely satisfying doing a little arm-work first thing.

Whisk the ricotta and egg yolk together until smooth, then whisk in the milk until you have a smooth, creamy mixture. Add the sugar (and the vanilla extract too, if using), lemon zest and salt, and then the flour and baking powder. Whisk well to get rid of any lumps.

Whisk the egg white in a separate bowl until you have soft peaks, then fold this gently into the batter, being careful not to knock out all of the air you have just incorporated.

Melt the butter in a frying pan (skillet) over a medium heat, then pour it into your batter mix and stir gently to combine.

Put the pan back over the heat and grease with a little oil. Spoon the mixture into the pan to form individual pancakes (in batches if necessary) and fry them for 1½ minutes or so on each side, until golden.

Serve with macerated strawberries, or some strawberry jam and yoghurt. They are also very good with honey and melted butter.

NOTE: If your ricotta is quite firm, use an electric beater to beat it until smooth, or whisk it well with a touch of the milk to loosen it; just to make sure there are no lumps in your final batter.

Boiled Eggs and Bottarga

Serves 2

2 very fresh eggs

bottarga, for grating

extra virgin olive oil (preferably Sardinian!), for drizzling

freshly ground black pepper or chilli (hot pepper) flakes (optional)

It makes pleasingly logical sense that one type of egg would be good with another, as that beloved fancy canapé of eggs with caviar proves. Here, the traditional tinned variety of deliciously fishy mini eggs to infuriatingly stick in the teeth and silkily melt on the tongue is replaced by Sardinia's own infamous 'caviar': bottarga.

I seem to spend a large part of my life banging on about bottarga, but I suppose there are worse drums to beat, because bottarga is underappreciated and deserves better. Bottarga in Italy is usually found in two forms: that made with the roe of tuna (from Sicily) and that made with the roe from mullet (Sardinia).

We live in one of the most important regions for bottarga production. The brackish lakes of nearby Cabras are where the mullet breed, and the sacks of roe from the females are removed, salted and cured to produce semi-hard amber lobes, which are sliced or grated accordingly. Sardinian bottarga is unlike any other: buttery, chewy, salty, bitter-sweet with notes of caramel, burnt butter and anchovy; it is one of the islands most important exports, and something that inspires much local pride. Its consistency is much softer than the Sicilian version, and its flavour much subtler. It is a rare and special treat, and surprisingly versatile. Think of it as like a fishy Parmesan and you have a good start for using it in recipes. It imparts intense depth and umami flavour to anything it is added to, and can be used both as an ingredient and a seasoning.

The most common way to eat bottarga in Sardinia is in thin slices on *pane carasau* drizzled with some of the local olive oil. It is also grated and melted into pasta dishes (usually a simple *spaghetti alla bottarga* or some sort of pasta with clams). It can be grated over cooked vegetables (broccoli, peas, potatoes and artichokes are all happy recipients) and on salads (tomato, celery, raw artichokes). It is delicious served alongside something creamy like burrata, mozzarella or ricotta. There are many things bottarga improves, and a little goes a long way, so although it is not cheap, you can stretch a lobe out over numerous meals and months.

The other natural companion for bottarga is eggs. Any variety of cooked egg works well: boiled (soft or hard), scrambled, fried or poached. The eggs' deep sunny richness reacts well to the salty caramel punch of bottarga and the colours are beautiful together too: amber on orange.

I like 5½- to 6-minute eggs with this, but if you like them runnier go for it – 4–5 minutes in boiling water is a runny yolk, by 6 it's more crème fraîche than double (heavy) cream consistency, and I prefer crème fraîche, especially as cutting them in half to serve is less messy.

Bring a small pan of water to the boil and carefully lower in your eggs. Boil for your preferred time, then run under cold water while peeling off the shells. Cut in half and serve with a generous grating of bottarga and a good drizzle of extra virgin olive oil. You can add a grind of black pepper or a pinch of chilli flakes, if you like.

Wild Leek Oozing Omelette

Makes 1 large or 2 individual omelettes (I only ever make omelettes for 1 or 2)

5–6 eggs (depending on hunger)

salt and pepper

a handful of wild leeks/ wild garlic or a spring onion (scallion), roughly chopped

2 tablespoons olive oil, plus extra as needed (or a nut of butter)

a little grated Parmesan

120 g (4 oz) stracchino or goat's cheese

some chopped herbs (parsley or chives) (optional but good)

When time is short and the refrigerator bare, eggs are forever your friend. I love an omelette for supper, and this is a particularly good one.

Stracchino is a cheese with a fluid identity, only just timidly solid, and the slightest heat makes it melt. Fittingly, as this is the sort of supper I make when I'm exhausted, the name *stracchino* is thought to derive from the Lombardian adjective *stracche*, which means 'tired', and described the cows after their long journey from up in the Alps down to the farms where this cheese was traditionally made. *Stracchino*, a tired cheese then, but a good one, with a very slight sourness and a wonderfully creamy, oozing texture. If you can't find it, try your favourite soft, lemony goat's cheese or ricotta.

Break the eggs into a bowl and whisk with a fork briefly, then mix in a splash of cold water and whisk until smooth. Season well with salt and pepper and set aside.

Wilt your leeks/wild garlic/spring onion in the olive oil in a frying pan (skillet) until just tender. Add a little more oil or a nut of butter to the pan, then pour in the eggs. Sprinkle over the grated Parmesan, scratch the eggs around a bit and then allow them to cook untouched creating a smooth underlayer. Blob over the stracchino/goat's cheese. Fold your omelette over in half, just once, while still a little liquid and oozy in the middle, then serve immediately, scattered with the chopped herbs, if using.

Repeat for the second one. Or, if you have a pan large enough, make a big one and cut it in half to serve.

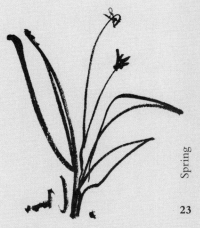

Salad of Endive, Soft Egg, Tuna, Olive and Potato with Creamy Anchovy Dressing

Serves 4

For the dressing

1 egg yolk

1½ teapoons red wine vinegar

2 anchovy fillets

about 150 ml (5 fl oz/generous ½ cup) extra virgin olive oil

½ teaspoon capers

1 tablespoon tuna (from a jar or tin)

salt, to taste

juice of 1 lemon, or to taste

For the salad

1 head of endive

5 boiled potatoes, roughly chopped

½ jar or tin of good tuna, about 70–100g (2½ –3½ oz) (optional)

a handful of black olives, pitted

a few capers (if you like them – I do)

a few leaves of parsley, roughly chopped

3 soft-boiled eggs (boiled for 6 minutes in boiling water, then peeled), halved

This is a sort of hybrid of *Niçoise* and *tonnato*; a happy meeting of North meets South. It is the perfect salad, as far as I am concerned; just a little bitter, sharp, punchy, creamy, sweet and sour. A more wintery version than the inescapably summery *Niçoise*, which is welcome on the first nights when it doesn't feel too bitter to eat just a salad for supper. This is light and fresh but still substantial enough to be winter fuel.

The dressing can be made in a blender and everything else takes a manner of minutes to put together. If I have a spare minute, I often boil potatoes without necessarily knowing what to do with them as they are so useful to have ready to throw into things, especially salads like this. Serve with grilled bread drizzled with oil.

Make the dressing in a blender (or use a stick blender, if you prefer). Start with the egg yolks, vinegar and anchovies, and blitz until smooth. Now add the oil in a drizzle, blitzing until thick. Blitz in the capers and tuna, then taste for seasoning and add salt and lemon juice as necessary. It should be adequately punchy to cut through the fat of the eggs and the sweet earthiness of the potatoes.

Arrange the endive leaves on a serving platter, then dot over the chunked potatoes and some pieces of tuna (if using). Next, sprinkle over the olives and/or capers, and the parsley, then top with the eggs. Drizzle over the dressing generously, adding a pot of the remainder alongside for dunking. Serve with some bruschetta.

Artichoke and Pecorino Lasagne

Serves 6

Almost every meal in Italy – at least in our household, involves
a fierce and fiery polemic about how and why certain dishes should
be made in certain ways. This specific lasagne inspired a particularly
hot and bubbling debate, as I had seen it made by a Sardinian woman
on YouTube and when she had cut a piece great strings of cheese had
stretched nearly a foot long as she levered the quivering slice out of its
molten bed and put it on a plate. As she took a bite, she declared with
unabashed pride, 'Well, it doesn't get better than this.'

Her self-belief and the foot-long strings of cheese were enough
to make me want to make this immediately, though I have eaten it
in various households in the last few years and often thought how
good it was. When made well, I think it is almost better than a classic
lasagne, but it needs to be almost criminally cheesy, as there is no ragù
to speak of, and the artichokes remain relatively subtle, so the gentle
flavours of béchamel and nutty artichoke need to be bolstered by
some prolific and powerful cheeses.

I have to say that making your own pasta makes a difference.
I never believed it until I did it myself, and the texture is totally
different. Making it as my Sardinian lady did in her video, the pasta is
also slightly thicker than the standard bought lasagne sheets, and this
makes the pasta more of a presence (and a welcome one at that).

I make it in three layers, which is ample, and less work for you,
after all the various preparation. I also make it in a disposable foil
container – as my Sardinian friends do, to save on washing-up (you
can recycle it after, but no scrubbing of crusted corners). Nevertheless,
even with shortcuts there can be no denying that making lasagne –
any sort of lasagne – is a labour of love. I make this in the last days
before Christmas, as a special frosty evening treat, or for Valentine's
Day, perhaps. The first artichokes start appearing in Sardinia in
November and carry on right through until April. They are loyal
winter companions. There is no getting around it, it is almost a
half-day's work, especially if you make the pasta yourself. But it is
pleasant work, on a Sunday perhaps, between baking your Christmas
cake and wrapping a few Christmas presents.

If you can't get artichokes, a mixture of spinach and mushrooms
is a very good substitute and has a similarly nutty and vegetal flavour.

For the artichokes

8–10 artichokes

3 tablespoons olive oil

2 whole garlic cloves, peeled

a handful of chopped parsley

1 glass of dry white wine
(no need to be exact)

1 glass of water

salt and pepper

For the pasta (or use
ready-made lasagne sheets)

300 g (10½ oz/scant 2½ cups)
semola (semolina), plus extra
for dusting

small pinch of salt

140–150 ml (4½–5 fl oz/
generous ½–scant ⅔ cup)
warm water

For the béchamel

100 g (3½ oz) butter

3 heaped tablespoons plain
(all-purpose) or '00' flour

800 ml (27 fl oz/generous
3 cups) whole milk

salt and pepper

½ teaspoon grated nutmeg

For the cheese

300 g (10½ oz) grated cheese
(a mixture of aged pecorino,
Parmesan and a younger cow's
milk cheese, like Casizolu or
Provolone, or Cheddar)

Cut the artichoke stalks about 2.5 cm (1 in) from the head (if nice and tender these are also edible). Peel away the outermost leaves and discard, then trim up the base with a knife/peeler. Cut the top (spiky part) of the leaves away leaving a neat head and then cut in half down the centre. With a teaspoon scoop out the fluffy choke and discard, then cut them into pieces. Use immediately so they don't turn brown.

Warm the olive oil in a sauté pan and begin to fry the artichokes along with the garlic for a few minutes until the garlic begins taking on colour and smelling good, then throw in the parsley, the wine and a good pinch of salt. Keep cooking and stirring until the wine has mostly bubbled off, then add the water and continue to cook, stirring occasionally, until the artichokes are tender and juicy (you may need a splash more wine or water to achieve this as you go). Season to taste.

Meanwhile, make your pasta dough. In a bowl, mix the *semola* and salt. Make a well in the middle and pour in the water, then bring everything together as one solid mass. Knead on a clean surface until smooth (a good few minutes), then wrap in cling film (plastic wrap) and allow to rest for at least 20-30 minutes.

Preheat the oven to 180°C (350°F/gas 4).

While the pasta rests make your béchamel. Melt the butter in a deep saucepan until bubbling, then add the flour, stir well with a whisk and allow to cook for a couple of minutes until it smells of digestive biscuits. Now add the milk, glug by glug, whisking all the time. Season with plenty of salt, pepper and freshly grated nutmeg. Once smooth and creamy, test again for seasoning and then set aside.

Now divide your pasta lump into three and roll out each piece to 2-3 mm (⅛ in) thick, dusting with extra *semola* if necessary. Place the first layer of pasta in a medium lasagne dish, then scatter over some of your artichoke mixture, a layer of béchamel and a third of the cheese. Repeat twice more, finishing with the remaining cheese – it's good to be generous with the cheese on top too, for extra golden bubblingness.

Cook in the oven for around 45 minutes until golden. Allow to sit for a couple of minutes and then serve, with a simple rocket (arugula) and lemon salad for after.

WILD
ASPARAGUS

Seek and ye shall find

After the first February rain showers, wild asparagus sprouts eagerly out of the ground; tall, spindly and single-minded.

If they are left unpicked, the spears can grow as tall as me. There is little danger of this, as these scrawny, purple-tinged shoots have the power to lure even the most reluctant forager out of his armchair and into the field. We spy cars parked in lay-bys, hesitant husbands and determined wives sliding down banks and snapping off spears, plastic bags in hands. On a warm spring afternoon I see my neighbour meandering homewards with a fat bunch squeezed in one hand, his flat cap dusty in the evening light, a wayward grass seed or two clinging to its fabric.

They are elusive, even to a keen hunter as I've become. I complain of a poor crop to Mauro, my counsel for all things *campagna*.

'You're just not looking hard enough.' He grins.

That evening it rains. Mauro looks out at the fat, warm drops bouncing off the veranda. The cats huddle in the orange trees.

'Tomorrow there'll be asparagus,' he says, almost to himself.

The next morning I set off. I look for the tell-tale bush; the indicator. The spears are so thin they're easy to miss even to a trained eye, but they grow out of a 'mother' plant; a fern-like, spiky, squat little bush. See this bush (an asparagus of yore that has grown unchecked) and close by you'll spot a

spear, perhaps so newly sprouted it is only an inch or so out of the ground, perfectly pointed, fat and dark purple. As it grows taller it becomes as skinny as a grasshopper's back legs, sprouting little buds either side, becoming tougher to eat too. The newly sprouted spears are the best; the most tender and sweet, but by default we pick a mixture of both.

The first shoots come in late February, and we forage for them right until May. Often they poke out from among the prickly pears. Just like the brambling of my youth, there were always thorny issues to deal with, nothing good was ever gained without a little suffering.

Thinner than their cultivated cousins, with a deep violet hue and a pungent, concentrated flavour they have a background bitterness that is beguiling and – to me at least – more appealing. Their flavour is deep and delicious, a little truffle-like, with nutty notes, a salinity and a whiff of hedge. A fixed part of the Mediterranean scrub, common in Sicily too, in Sardinia it is a rite of passage hunting for handfuls in early spring.

Anything that you can do with store-bought asparagus you can do with wild asparagus, but here, as so often the shoots tend to be a little tougher, there is little tradition of eating them lightly boiled *al dente*, and stronger arguments for braising or sautéing. These are some of my favourite ways to prepare them.

Spring

Malloreddus with Wild Asparagus

Serves 2 as a primo

about 150–200 g (5–7 oz) asparagus

200 g (7 oz) pasta of your choice (I use *malloreddus*)

4 tablespoons olive oil, or as needed

1 small white onion, finely sliced

1 small dried red chilli, crumbled, or a pinch of chilli (hot pepper) flakes

3 or 4 small, sweet tomatoes, diced (optional)

splash of white wine (optional)

40 g (1½ oz) butter

40 g (1½ oz) Parmesan or pecorino, finely grated, plus extra to serve

salt, to taste

fresh marjoram, to garnish (optional)

One of the best ways of cooking wild asparagus that I know, here the spears are braised down to a rich, pond-green mulch into which plentiful butter and Parmesan is melted, and then used to coat pasta.

If you cannot find wild asparagus, cultivated is fine – just try to choose English, skinnier stems.

As this involves a foraged ingredient, and I never know how much I can get hold of, I adjust this recipe accordingly. If you have a healthy quantity of asparagus and want to taste it in its purity, by all means leave out the tomato.

First wash your asparagus well. Cut it into 2.5 cm (1 in) pieces and set any woody ends aside.

Put a pot of salted water on to boil for the pasta, adding the discarded woody bits of the asparagus to flavour it. Once boiling, fish out the asparagus ends and then drop in the pasta. Cook the pasta until it is just *al dente*.

Meanwhile, heat the olive oil in a sauté pan over a medium heat and sweat the onion, asparagus and chilli for a good 10-15 minutes or so, until soft and beginning to fall apart. Add a splash of water and continue to cook down, slowly, until the asparagus is almost completely soft. Add the tomatoes and cook again until everything is mushy and the asparagus is completely tender, adding a little extra oil or water if necessary (you can add a splash of white wine here, if you prefer). Taste and season with salt.

Drain the pasta, reserving a little of the cooking water. Add the butter to the sauce, along with the drained pasta and the Parmesan/pecorino. Add a little pasta cooking water and continue to cook for a minute or so, stirring gently, until the sauce is creamy and coating the pasta evenly. Serve, sprinkled with extra cheese and a few marjoram sprigs (if using).

You can make this without the tomatoes and cook the asparagus less for a fresher flavour and to keep the spears intact, if you prefer.

Variation: Wild Asparagus and Bottarga Pasta by Luigi

An excellent dish I ate made by my honey-making friend Luigi. Follow the recipe for the asparagus pasta above, leaving out the tomato. Once you have drained the pasta and added it to the pan with the braised asparagus, add 3 tablespoonfuls of finely grated bottarga and a little extra water. Stir and toss well until creamy, season and serve.

Wild Asparagus Omelette

Serves 1 as a solitary supper or 2 as a snack with other bits

This is Lorenzo's family's favourite way of preparing asparagus, which involves just two perfect, spring ingredients: a very good egg, fresh from the hen, and some home-gathered asparagus. We make it less omelette-y and more asparagus-y, so you can really taste it. Sardinians treat wild asparagus with the same reverence Tuscans treat truffles; never to be tampered with by taste-altering tricks or added accoutrements. The egg binds everything together and provides a rich and buttery canvas.

1 tablespoon olive oil

large handful of wild asparagus, cut into short lengths

4 very fresh eggs

salt and pepper

Heat the oil in a sauté pan and begin to sauté your asparagus. Add a splash of water or two, if necessary, and cook until just tender.

Whisk the eggs loosely in a bowl with a fork, season them well and then pour into the mixture. Turn over once, leave a little gooey in the middle, and serve as a perfect morsel before the main meal.

Wild Asparagus Risotto

Serves 2

One of the few occasions where I (almost) prefer rice to pasta, the slow-cooked asparagus lends an almost mushroomy quality to an otherwise classically creamy risotto. The colours of a pond, but the flavours of paradise.

2 tablespoons butter, plus 30 g (1 oz) to finish

2 tablespoons olive oil, plus extra for drizzling

½ sweet white onion, diced

180 g (6 oz) asparagus (roughly 2 small bunches), washed, woody bits removed and cut into short lengths

180 g (6 oz/generous ¾ cup) risotto rice

1 small glass of dry white wine or Vernaccia

about 1 litre (34 fl oz/4 cups) chicken or vegetable stock, warm

50 g (2 oz) pecorino, finely grated

salt, to taste

Warm the 2 tablespoons of butter and the olive oil in a deep saucepan and sauté the onion with the asparagus until both are soft and the onion is translucent. Add a splash of water now and then if things look like they'll catch. It will take a good 15-20 minutes until things get soft and slippery.

Add the rice and stir for a minute or so. Add the glass of wine and cook over a medium heat for a few minutes, stirring and allowing the alcohol to boil off. Now add a ladleful of the stock and stir until it has been absorbed into the rice. Repeat the process, ladle by ladle, stirring after each addition until the rice absorbs the liquid. Once your rice is *al dente* and the liquid has mostly evaporated, remove from the heat for the *mantecatura*, or 'creaming'.

With a wooden spoon, beat in the second amount of butter along with the grated pecorino. Beat well for a minute or two until a luscious creamy sauce is formed. Add salt to taste. When you are happy with the seasoning, serve in a puddle in a bowl, with a drizzle of oil on top.

Broad Beans, Bottarga and Ricotta

Serves 2

This is the perfect sort of clever but instant/ impressive lunch dish that requires only bread, and preferably no cutlery. I eat it with my fingers.

The bottarga provides salt, the beans sweet, green nuttiness, and the creamy ricotta rounds everything off perfectly. It is based on a Simon Hopkinson recipe that uses thin slices of cured cod's roe. If you can't get hold of bottarga, then this would be a good substitute. And if you can't get hold of any cured fish roe then good prosciutto would be an excellent replacement. The important thing is to have something salty.

Be generous with your oil here, and use top-quality oil. The beans are best young and tender, and thus don't need blanching.

about 30 g (1 oz) bottarga/cod's roe, or a few slices of good prosciutto

large handful of small tender broad (fava) beans

about 60 g (2 oz) fresh ricotta

To serve

herbs/chive flowers

plentiful good-quality olive oil

pane carasau or toasted ciabatta/sourdough

Slice the bottarga and then arrange all three elements prettily on a serving platter. Scatter with herbs/chive flowers if you like, and then drizzle abundantly with your best olive oil. Serve with good crisp bread (pane carasau) or with some toasted ciabatta/sourdough, drizzled with more oil.

Bashed Broad Beans with Ricotta, Herbs and Lemon on Bruschetta

Serves 2 as a snack/light lunch

These can make rather elegant little nibbles/ canapés, if you are so inclined, but I live in a world notably devoid of canapés so prefer to serve them as a simple antipasti or light lunch. I like to use *pane carasau*, which has the perfect crisp consistency, but if you cannot get hold of it toasting/grilling (broiling)/roasting some good bread will be an excellent substitute. Make sure it is nice and crisp, and drizzle it with good olive oil before piling on your bean mash.

80 g (3 oz) or so of young, podded broad (fava) beans

40 g (1½ oz) fresh ricotta

30 g (1 oz) Parmesan, grated

4 tablespoons olive oil, plus extra to serve

zest and juice of ½ large lemon

handful of herbs (such as mint, parsley, wild fennel or dill, tarragon, chervil, chives), plus extra to serve

salt, to taste

bruschetta/toast/crisp bread, to serve

Bash the beans in a pestle and mortar or blitz briefly in a food processor until you have a rough pulp. Mix in the other ingredients and taste for seasoning, adjusting accordingly.

Serve on bruschetta/toast/crisp bread garnished with more herbs and extra oil.

Basic Egg Pasta Dough

Serves 1

100 g (3½ oz/generous ¾ cup) *semola* (semolina)

1 egg

There was a time when I wrote recipes for a much more complicated type of pasta dough with egg yolks and whole eggs and soft wheat flour in different quantities. Now I have experimented more and found the true, pure egg pasta dough recipe, which like so many things in life, was there all along in its understated simplicity.

There is nothing in life more satisfying than a ratio recipe, and this egg pasta provides the sort of perfect symmetry Da Vinci would be proud of. If you cannot get hold of *semola* (semolina) easily you can use '00' flour or plain (all-purpose) flour but according to Sardinian tradition I like to use *semola*, as all pastas, breads and doughs were made with the hard-grain wheat before the arrival of soft wheat varieties.

Semola gives the cooked pasta a more chewy and satisfying texture, and a more golden hue. If you use very good eggs it will make a difference too. You will taste it in the flavour and smell it in your dough. Once mixed the dough has a perfume that is so specific I sometimes want to make it for this reason alone. Unlike a simple *semola*-and-water pasta it starts sticky, but with a little work (your hands, bowl and surfaces should become miraculously clean) you should end up with a silky, supple, sun-yellow dough, which is pure sensual pleasure to both sniff, touch and squeeze.

This makes a generous single portion, and once made you can decide what shape to cut it into, if not the pappardelle/ribbons opposite. My favourites are – unsurprisingly – the less demanding ones, something like *maltagliati* (meaning 'badly cut', these are sort of little rhomboid pasta rags) or *fazzoletti* (larger hankerchief/tissue-shaped pieces).

You will need a bowl (I like a terracotta one traditional to Sardinia called a *xivedda*), a wooden board/surface to work on, and your hands. That is all.

Place the *semola* in the bowl and add the egg to the centre. Using the tips of your fingers start to stir, breaking the egg and using your fingertips in a whisking motion to mix everything together. Once the mixture begins to form large flakes you can start to press and knead the dough with your hands and bring it together to form a rough lump. Now remove it from the bowl, set the bowl aside somewhere and start to knead properly on your clean work surface. Knead well and fairly vigorously, pushing the dough away from you with the heel of your hand and then rolling it back inwards. Turn the dough slightly and repeat the process. You should end up with a smooth, silky lump of dough with no dry or flaky bits. The beauty of making pasta is that it is the opposite of making pastry, none of the nerve-wracking delicacy. Pasta dough likes to be treated with force. Use the dough to pummel out your frustrations of the day.

Wrap the dough in cling film (plastic wrap) and leave to rest at room temperature for at least 20 minutes. Now it is ready to shape.

Egg Pasta Ribbons with Marscarpone, Lemon, Mint and Broad Beans

Serves 2 generously

For the pasta

200 g (7 oz/generous 1½ cups) *semola* (semolina)

2 eggs

For the sauce

4 tablespoons mascarpone

3–4 tablespoons grated Parmesan

zest of 1 small lemon and a little of its juice

a handful of parsley, mint, wild fennel and or marjoram, roughly chopped

a couple of handfuls of small, fresh broad (fava) beans

a good glug of extra virgin olive oil

salt, to taste

If there are two more emblematic images of Italy than fresh laundry neatly pegged and pasta drying in the sun, then I cannot think of them. *Panni* (laundry) and pasta are fundamental parts of everyday life. A place as meticulously neat as Italy and as blessed with regular sunshine could not fail to be devoted to the art of laundry, and an art it is. This is a place where even children's stuffed toys are laundered and hung up neatly by their ears to dry. For my mother-in-law Monica, *stendere i panni* is a way of relaxing after a hard day's work teaching unruly teenagers. Aside from the infamous Neopolitan laundry lines, one of the most striking Italian images I remember ever seeing is from the fifties – a black and white photo of row upon row of spaghetti drying in the sun. I cannot help thinking of this whenever I hang out my laundry; the rhythmic mirroring of pasta and *panni*.

These pasta ribbons are a sort of pappardelle that don't take themselves too seriously. Officially pappardelle are flat, broad strips of egg pasta dough, fatter than tagliatelle, which derive their name from the word *pappare*, a colloquial way of saying 'to eat'. I cut them so fat I'm not sure a true Tuscan would even allow them to be called that, so I loosely call them ribbons. They are incredibly satisfying and somehow sensual to eat, folding and flopping in the mouth like great, flat fish, giving the occasional eggy slap to the cheek or chin as they are manoeuvred mouthwards. They are also instantly beautiful, tumbling yellow ribbons on a plate, and they feel to me – given that they are such a celebration of the egg – perfectly suited to this light and lemony spring combination.

If you don't want to make your own pappardelle or don't have time to, you can easily buy dried/ready-made, or even buy ready-made fresh pasta sheets and cut them into thick strips. This is one of those wonderful pasta dishes in which the sauce can be made in the time that the pasta takes to cook (and in this case, even less).

Make the pasta dough according to the instructions opposite.

In a bowl, mix the mascarpone with the Parmesan, lemon zest and a good squeeze of its juice. Season well with salt and add most of the chopped herbs. Taste and adjust accordingly.

Bring a deep pan of water to the boil, add the pasta and cook until just *al dente* (this will take only a couple of minutes). Cook the beans at the same time in the same water. If they are fresh and small they should take the same time as the pasta, just a minute or two; if you are using dried pasta you will need to wait until just a minute away from it being *al dente* to toss in your beans. Drain, reserving some of the pasta cooking water.

Let the mascarpone down with a little of the reserved pasta water, and then toss everything back in the pan and stir until creamy. Add the olive oil and stir/toss again until shiny and creamy. Taste and adjust for seasoning and serve with some extra herbs sprinkled on top.

Fried Acacia Flowers

Serves 6

For the batter

around 140 ml (4½ fl oz/ generous ½ cup) sparkling water

80 g (3 oz/¾ cup) '00' flour

a pinch of salt

1–2 ice cubes

12 heads of acacia flowers (robinia) (2 per person)

mild olive oil, grapeseed or sunflower oil, for deep frying

To serve

fragrant honey

orange zest/orange blossom water (optional)

In late April, the worst months are past and *feste* are falling like blossom. Days brighten and the sky begins to ache once again with that famous blue. The cat yawns in a sunbeam and we feel the widening, an uncurling, unfurling awakening of Spring. The air is heady with the scent of orange blossom, the distant buzz of bees and tractors. Mauro is muddier than usual; he is ploughing the vineyards. A great brave single asparagus spear, self-seeded in a flower pot, shoots up to a metre tall; the heavy rains and subsequent sunshine are perfect for growth spurts.

The almond blossom that lined the lanes has given way to heavy white clusters of false acacia; small trees made up of fine, delicate and haphazard branches, hidden spines and heavy dangling, blousy bunches of white flowers. The false acacia, 'black locust' or *Robinia pseudoacacia*, is a small tree that looks a bit like a white wisteria. It has pale green, pebble-shaped leaves and delicate white flowers that hang in dense and drooping, haphazard tumbles, which batter each other in the breeze. It is, in fact, a part of the same family as wisteria (*Fabaceae/ Faboideae*) and is a relative of peas and beans, all of which have similarly fragrant and frequently edible flowers, with the same slightly pouting, fish-lipped blooms.

These white blossoms have an ethereal scent; a little like orange blossom, a little like honey and vanilla and not far from jasmine; their flavour is a fainter version of this perfume. Daintily deep-fried and eaten with an extra drizzle of honey they are truly ambrosial. They make a lovely starter or pudding for a spring lunch. You can serve them with a little extra orange blossom water/fresh orange zest to highlight the flavour, if you like.

Make the batter by gently whisking the water into the flour and salt. Add the last drop of water slowly and mix very gently, to maintain the fizz (this makes a nice, crisp, light batter). The consistency should be like pouring cream. Add an ice cube or two (again, this helps keep things crisp).

Meanwhile, gently wash the flowers and lay out to dry.

Bring a deep pan of oil to frying temperature (around 180–190°C/ 350–375°F, it should begin to swirl but not smoke). Have some paper towels ready.

Delicately dunk the flower heads into the batter, shaking gently to remove excess batter.

Dunk them, holding their stems, into the hot oil, shaking as they go in, to allow the flowers to splay and excess batter to shake off into the oil. Fry for a minute or two until golden, then drain on paper towels.

To serve, drizzle with honey and sprinkle with a few drops of orange blossom water and some grated orange zest, if you like.

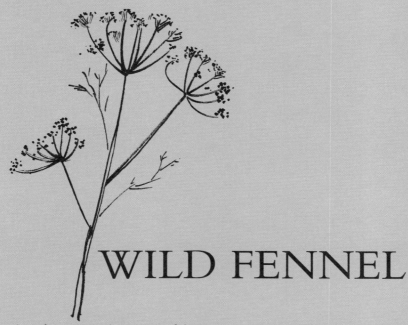

WILD FENNEL

In early spring, the *potatura* (pruning) of the vines begins. Mauro heads off with his habitual plastic bucket for *campagna*, complete with secateurs, little sharp knives (continually robbed from Monica's knife drawer, much to her irritation), nameless bits of string and battered old bottle of water.

Early one spring evening, just as the setting sun begins to cast shadows over the silver artichokes in the field next door, I pass the vineyard. He takes his scissors and gives a few careful and considered snips here and there, cutting the tangled tendrils to tidy stumps, leaving on each branch three nodules from the base, out of which sprout tiny green buds. Then he begins to clear around the base of each vine, and digs me up a root of wild fennel, which

grows like a weed here, its tell-tale feathery fronds spread through field and hedgerow. The root, unlike cultivated fennel, is slender and mostly green rather than white. He strips it of the woody outer layers with his knife until there is just a pale green, succulent root. He encourages me to take a bite.

'This was the original *merenda* [snack] of the wine maker,' he says. 'When you're pruning all day, there is nothing better.'

I take a bite of the root. It is sweet and also surprisingly salty, minerally, and with that undeniable liquorice undercurrent. I can imagine it in a salad, a mayonnaise, with strawberries, oranges, olives, asparagus. But eaten like this, as the *merenda* of the pruner, it has its own magic too.

Spaghetti with Garlic Breadcrumbs, Anchovies, Chilli, Wild Fennel and Lemon

Serves 2 as a main course

200 g (7 oz) spaghetti/
linguine/bucatini

6 tablespoons extra virgin olive
oil, plus extra to serve

60 g (2 oz) bread (best with
sourdough/ciabatta or focaccia),
blitzed to crumbs in a
food processor

2 garlic cloves, finely sliced

8 anchovy fillets

good pinch of dried chilli (hot
pepper) flakes

zest of 1 small lemon

a few fronds of wild fennel,
finely chopped, plus extra
to serve

salt, to taste

Breadcrumbs are everyday magic. The only thing better than fresh crusty bread is crispy fried breadcrumbs, or fat toasted croutons, chewy inside and fat-soaked and crisp on the outside. If you are lucky enough to have leftover bread don't ever throw it away. Guard it closely; it is precious kitchen treasure. This is something every Italian cook knows well. Stale bread can form both the base and substance of many a classic Italian dish, from *ribollita* to *panzanella*. In such dishes, it is not always simply a filler or a texture-giver, it's often the best bit of the whole dish. When you're eating a *panzanella*, for example, is it the tomatoes you're fighting for, or the chunks of chewy, oil-soaked bread?

In this classic dish, loosely based around the Sicilian *spaghetti con la mollica*, golden, garlicky crumbs provide both nutty, toasty flavour and crunchy texture, and replace the need for grated cheese (in Sicily they were often referred to as poor man's cheese). The addition of wild fennel is something often seen in Sicily, where it grows as prolifically as here in Sardinia. It adds a wonderful sweet herbal element to the dish, but if you can't find it use a handful of chopped parsley.

Bring a pan of well-salted water to the boil and drop in your pasta.

Meanwhile, heat half of the oil in a heavy saucepan. Drop in the crumbs and fry, stirring continuously over a medium heat until golden all over (about 5 minutes). Scrape out the crumbs, leaving them to drain a little on a piece of paper towel.

Wipe out the pan and add the second batch of oil. Fry the sliced garlic for a minute until lightly golden. Add the anchovies and stir them well until they melt. Remove from the heat, then add the chilli flakes, lemon zest and chopped fennel.

When the spaghetti is cooked (usually aim for 2 minutes less than the packet instructions), drain it, reserving a small cup of the cooking water. Add the spaghetti to the pan with the sauce and place it back over the heat. Add a good splash of the cooking water and toss the pasta until you get a good amount of shining sauce. If it looks dry, add a little more oil or a litte more water. Once you're happy and things look slick and juicy, taste and adjust the seasoning, then add the crumbs, a slosh more oil if desired and toss once again.

Plate and finish with an extra drizzle of oil and a few extra fennel fronds, if you like. Have a large glass of wine.

Instant Ricotta Doughnuts with Saffron and Blood Orange

Makes around 10–12

2 eggs

250 g (9 oz) ricotta

3 tablespoons sugar

good pinch of salt

grated zest of 1 lemon and
2 blood oranges

100 g (3½ oz/generous ¾ cup)
plain (all-purpose) flour

50 g (2 oz/scant ½ cup) potato
flour (optional but helps make
them extra light – can swap
for plain/all-purpose flour
if preferred)

2 teaspoons baking powder
or ½ sachet of Italian *lievito*
(usually flavoured with vanilla)

½ teaspoon vanilla extract
(optional and if not using *lievito*)

good pinch of saffron threads,
soaked in 1 tablespoon warm
water, or a pinch of
ground saffron

1 litre (34 fl oz/4 cups) frying
oil (I use groundnut, peanut
or sunflower)

sugar, either granulated or icing
(confectioners'), for dusting
(or honey, if you prefer)

'Instant doughnuts' has a whiff of the impossible about it, the sort of thing a YouTube advert might shout at you from the corner of your screen as you harmlessly search for cushion covers. Nevertheless, instant doughnuts are what these are; soft, golden nuggets of the incredible made edible.

In Sardinia these are known as *arrubiolus*, which is derived from the word *arrubio*, meaning red, in tribute to the deep sunset orange they acquire inside from the saffron, and their red-golden finished appearance when fried. Flamingos, which fleck the Sardinian skyline and glow pink in turquoise lakes near us in Oristano, are known as *sa genti arrubia*, or 'the red people'. The sight of their long-legged forms flying overhead, with their black-tipped wings, fuschia-pink bodies and toucan-like cartoon beaks is one I will never tire of.

The idea is straightforward: a simple batter lightened by baking powder, deep-fried, then dusted in sugar. The traditional flavourings are orange or lemon zest, and the saffron is a firmly Sardinian addition. The batter is essentially cake-mix consistency. Two spoons scoop it neatly into hot frying oil – in they plop, up they bob, out they come; golden and glistening. Fried cakes, small and sweet and perfumed, and wonderfully light, they stay moist for days if you keep them in an airtight container.

Whisk the eggs and ricotta until smooth. Add the sugar, salt, citrus zest, flour/s, baking powder/*lievito*, vanilla extract (if using) and saffron, and whisk until you have a smooth batter.

Heat the oil in a deep pan until it swirls (it must be around 190°C/375°F, but not so hot that it's smoking, otherwise it will burn the *frittelle*). Test it with a piece of bread if you like: the bread should bob and fry nicely, becoming brown after 30 seconds or so.

Using two teaspoons, scoop little blobs of the mixture into the hot oil (they should be the size of walnuts and will swell slightly while cooking). Turn them over as they cook to make sure they are evenly brown on all sides. Scoop them out onto some paper towels, then roll them in the sugar of your choice while still hot. They are also very good drizzled with honey, if you prefer.

Zeppole di San Giuseppe
Choux Buns with Cream and Sour Cherries
Makes 6–8

For the pastry

50 g (2 oz) butter

a pinch of salt

250 ml (8½ fl oz/1 cup) water

150 g (5 oz/1¼ cups) plain (all-purpose) or '00' flour

4 good eggs

For the cream

250 ml (8½ fl oz/1 cup) double (heavy) cream

2 tablespoons icing (confectioners') sugar

a few drops of vanilla extract/ scraped seeds from ½ pod (optional)

To finish

Fabbri Amarena Sour Cherries

icing (confectioners') sugar, for dusting

Poor Giuseppe (Joseph) tends to get overlooked in all the Madonna (Mary) worship, though he is a character close to my heart as my brother always played him – somewhat reluctantly – in the Nativity, and as his commemorative *dolce* is one of my favourites. Little is known or written about the first-century Jewish carpenter named Giuseppe who unwittingly became the father of Christ, and then became venerated as a saint in the Catholic church; the patron saint of workers whose *festa* falls on 19th March. This is the Italian Father's Day, Giuseppe being the archetypal father.

Zeppole are generally a sort of deep-fried doughnut-style food (more often shaped in spirals or piped), which crop up in various shapes and sizes for traditional festivities all over Italy. Those associated with San Giuseppe are special in that they contain thick, yellow pastry cream and are topped with a glossy sour cherry. The pastry itself is not a yeasted dough but a choux pastry, and is sometimes fried, but this is one occasion where I opt for baking over frying.

So often mistakes make the best recipes, and while tradition calls for a thick yellow pastry cream filling, I had used all my best eggs in the choux, so made a simple sweetened whipped cream, and as the choux is so wonderfully eggy itself this was pronounced better than the original. Mauro, our in-house, quiet and saintly father figure, said that it made the sour cherry positively explosive, set against such a delicate background, rather than a sweet and cloying custard cream. This is one occasion where I am anti-custard, and it does make the making of them easier/quicker too. If you want to stick with tradition, follow the pastry cream recipe on p.56.

These are best eaten the day they are made. You can easily freeze the choux once cooked and fill them on another occasion.

Preheat the oven to 200°C (400°F/gas 6).

For the pastry, warm the butter, salt and water in a saucepan and bring just to the boil, then add the flour and whisk over a medium heat. Continue stirring over a medium heat for a few minutes until the paste is smooth and shiny and comes away from the edges of the pan in one uniform lump. Remove from the heat, transfer to a bowl and allow to cool.

Beat the eggs in a bowl. Once your flour paste has cooled, beat in the eggs a little at a time (this will take quite a lot of arm work, or you can use an electric beater) until you have a smooth, shiny paste. Decant the paste into a piping bag fitted with a fluted nozzle.

Line a baking tray (pan) with greaseproof paper and pipe circles of the pastry onto the tray. Bake for 25 minutes until golden and risen. Remove from the oven and leave to cool.

Whip the cream with the icing sugar and vanilla until soft peaks form.

Once cool, pipe the cream into the centre of the *zeppole*, then top with a sour cherry and dust with icing sugar. Serve.

PANIFICIO

PASTIFICIO

GASTRONOMIA

Torta Mimosa

Serves 8–10

As downy, yellow and innocent as an Easter chick, the Mimosa is a curious and captivating cake. Ethereally light, unapologetically creamy and sweet, it is aesthetically unique, covered with a daffodil-yellow furry-crumb coating designed to resemble sprays of mimosa.

Mimosa blooms at the very cusp of spring, usually the first few days of March, yellow sprays by the roadside either shining in the blithe spring sun or battered by fickle March winds. The cheering little pom-pom flowers the colour of scrambled egg have become the symbol for International Woman's Day, or *La Festa della Donna*, as it is called in Italy, where it is customary to give mothers, grandmothers, daughters, wives and girlfriends a small, yellow spray, heady with honey-sweet scent.

Dreamt up in Rieti in the 1950s, the enterprising pastry chef Adelmo Renzi entered his invention into a cake competition at Sanremo in 1962, which it won and thus achieved nationwide fame. (Once one knows the cake was a product of the fifties/sixties, it makes all the more aesthetic sense and justifies further the retro but delicious addition of tinned pineapple.) It is now used as a festive springtime celebration cake, most often associated with International Women's Day but also served at spring weddings and birthdays. Its simple but winning flavours are a perfect emblem of spring; lemon-scented custard and a simple, egg-rich sponge.

To achieve the most yellow results, make sure you opt for good eggs. I also add pineapple, which makes it extra fresh, light and floral tasting, and gives me a chance to rediscover a long-lost nostalgia for tinned pineapple, which works wonderfully in puddings – think of the classic upside-down cake. (I have also been fed a surprising white tiramisù once, which involved pineapple, and it is my life's ambition to recreate it.) Here, it accentuates the lemon and lightens the whole assembly beautifully.

Crema diplomatica is a simple pastry cream lightened and enriched with whipped cream, and the most wonderful filling for tarts and cakes. I make this two layers but you could easily double the recipe and go for four if it's a really special occasion, a party or wedding perhaps.

This is a wonderful assembly; light, simple, creamy and aesthetically unique, treading a dainty line between pudding and teatime (or breakfast) treat. It is also a cake that, due to its unbearable lightness of being and its slight soaking in pineapple, gives a little sigh when you cut into it. A cake with charisma.

N.B. This pineapple version is especially child-friendly, but if you want something a little more grown-up you can add some rum to your pineapple juice and paint the cake with that too.

Recipe continues overleaf

For the sponge

butter, for greasing

200 g (7 oz/1¾ cups) '00' flour, plus extra for dusting

5 eggs

200 g (7 oz/scant 1 cup) sugar

pinch of salt

a few drops of vanilla extract/ seeds from a vanilla pod

a sprig of mimosa, to decorate

For the crema diplomatica

4 egg yolks

80 g (3 oz/⅓ cup) sugar

40 g (1½ oz/⅓ cup) cornflour (cornstarch)

pinch of salt

500 ml (17 fl oz/2 cups) whole milk

a few strips of lemon zest

200 ml (7 fl oz/scant 1 cup) double (heavy)/whipping cream

2 tablespoons icing (confectioners') sugar

For the filling

1 x 140 g (4½ oz) tin pineapple in juice

Begin by making the sponge. Preheat the oven to 170°C (325°F/gas 3) and grease a deep-sided 20 cm (8 in) cake tin (pan) first with butter and then dust with a light sprinkling of flour.

Whisk the eggs and sugar with an electric beater until they have tripled in volume, are smooth, yellow and moussey, and the falling mixture holds its shape for a good few seconds when the whisk is lifted (this will take about 10 minutes of good whisking). Fold in the flour, sifting it in carefully, then gently fold in the salt and vanilla, making sure not to lose all of the air you have incorporated.

Decant the batter into your prepared tin, then bake for around 40 minutes until golden and just set. Remove and allow to cool in the tin.

Now make your *crema diplomatica*. Whisk the egg yolks, sugar, cornflour and salt together in a bowl until smooth. Heat the milk with the lemon zest until just at a scald, then whisk it into the egg mixture. Now return the whole lot to the pan and cook over a low heat, whisking continuously until you have a smooth cream the consistency of mayonnaise. Remove from the heat, take out the lemon strips and discard, and allow to cool completely.

Whip the cream with the icing sugar until you have stiff peaks, then fold into the cooled pastry cream.

Remove the cooled cake from the tin and slice it horizontally into three equal layers (you can use a cotton thread or a sharp, long serrated knife to do this). Place the bottom layer on a serving plate. The middle layer will become your 'fluffy' mimosa topping. Remove the outermost brown bits of the sponge and break the yellow inner sponge into small, pea-sized crumbs with your fingers.

Using a pastry brush, dampen the top and bottom layers of the cake with the juice from the pineapple, lightly anointing rather than soaking. Chop a few slices of the pineapple into small pieces and scatter over the bottom layer. Now spread around just under two-thirds of the *crema* over the bottom layer and place the top layer of sponge on top. Spread the rest of the *crema* around the sides and top of the cake and then cover in the crumbs, sticking them onto the *crema*.

Serve with a sprig of mimosa.

Keep in the refrigerator, covered, if you do not want to serve it immediately.

Blood Orange, Honey and Saffron Hot Cross Buns

Makes 10

We sit at the low table with the fruit-patterned tablecloth, mugs of *caffe latte* steaming before us and Lorenzo watches in awe-filled silence as the opaque slabs of butter melt into transparent pools on the craggy surface of a split and toasted hot cross bun. Fat raisins glint with expectation, some of them cut open to show wet brown insides, smudged into the dough where the bun has been sliced. There are orange flecks of homemade peel, tiny specks of nutmeg and cinnamon, a golden-brown hue of saffron and the scent of orange, honey, butter and spices. He cradles his mug of coffee and takes a bite of warm, buttered bun. Teeth sink into soft, scented dough, a raisin bursts in his mouth.

'Yes,' he says, exhaling softly, holding his bun up to the light like a holy relic. 'You English know about breakfast.'

These buns, though traditional in England for Good Friday, are welcome all year round without the crosses too; both children and adults adore them. They make a magnificent breakfast. The quantity of eggs and butter mean they are wonderfully rich, a truly enriched dough, but using all bread flour rather than plain (all-purpose) ensures they stay bready, too, rather than coming out as little cakes. Having said that they are perfectly edible untoasted and unbuttered, the choice is yours. I add no sugar, as I like the sweetness to come purely from the honey, which adds its own fragrant flavour too.

Although the recipe says make a 'starter', don't be put off; this is not something you have to mix up days, nights or hours in advance. It is good to leave it an hour to give the yeast a kick-start before you slow it down with all that butter, but it is not essential. I've been impatient and used it after 20 minutes and things have still worked out fine. Like sell-by dates, it's only advisory.

The saffron gives a delicious exotic whiff and adds a bit of Sardinia to this undoubtedly English Easter treat, as well as contributing to a rich golden colour. I urge you to use homemade candied peel. Commercial candied peel has no flavour and rubble-like texture. If you make your own it will make a world of difference. If you can't face it, just add the fresh zest of another orange and give yourself a break.

Recipe continues overleaf

170 g (6 oz/1⅓ cups) raisins

zest and juice of
2 blood oranges

For the starter

20 g (¾ oz) fresh yeast
(or 10 g/½ oz dried yeast)

120 g (4 oz/⅓ cup) honey

200 ml (7 fl oz/
scant 1 cup) warm water
(at body temperature)

220 g (8 oz/1¾ cups) strong
bread flour

½ teaspoon ground cinnamon

½ teaspoon ground nutmeg

¼ teaspoon ground saffron

¼ teaspoon ground cloves

For the final dough

400 g (14 oz/3⅓ cups) strong
bread flour

2 egg yolks

12 g (½ oz) salt

130 g (4 oz) butter,
cubed and softened

100 g (3½ oz/½ cup)
(homemade) candied peel,
drained and dried of any juice,
finely diced

For the cross

80 g (3 oz/scant ⅔ cup) plain
(all-purpose) flour

about 60 ml (2 fl oz/¼ cup)
water, or more as needed

pinch of salt

pinch of sugar

To finish

a little flavourless oil,
for greasing

milk, for brushing

honey, for glazing

Soak the raisins in the orange juice, allowing them to absorb it all and soften up (stir them occasionally and you will notice they plump and soften after 30 minutes or so).

For the starter, melt the yeast and honey in the warm water, whisking well to dissolve, and then whisk in all the remaining starter ingredients along with the orange zest. Cover and leave in a warm place for 1 hour.

Add the remaining ingredients for the final dough along with the starter to a stand mixer and mix until you have a smooth, even dough. This will take a fair amount of kneading/mixing. If doing this by hand, it will look a shaggy mess at first, but revel in the kneading process as it comes together as a fairly neat and smooth dough. It will be a little tacky, but don't worry. Leave to rise overnight in the refrigerator, well covered, or at room temperature for 1–1½ hours until doubled in size.

Using a dough scraper and lightly oiling your (digital) scales, work surface and hands with a little flavourless oil, cut and shape the dough into balls of 130 g (4 oz). Place the balls on a large baking tray (pan) lined with greaseproof paper an inch or so apart. Tuck them away somewhere warm and draught-free to keep them out of mischief. This could be inside the oven (turned off!) if you are short of space – as I am. Let them rise for 1–1½ hours until doubled in size (this stage can also be done overnight in the refrigerator).

Remove the buns from their safe place and preheat the oven to 180°C (350°F/gas 4).

Use a pastry brush to brush the buns evenly with milk.

Mix the ingredients for the cross together in a bowl. Make a little piping bag out of greaseproof paper or use a piping bag with a small nozzle and decant the mixture into it. Pipe the cross on top of each bun.

Bake in the oven for 14–16 minutes until golden brown. Remove from the oven and glaze, while still warm, with a pastry brush dipped in honey.

Eat as they are (these buns are good enough to be eaten alone) or split, toasted and topped with slabs of salty butter.

NOTES: Make sure the butter is taken out of the refrigerator in good time and softens nicely, otherwise it won't mix evenly into the dough. This is particularly important if you are mixing by hand. If you are mixing by machine it matters less, as the force of the machine will help break down the butter and incorporate it. A dough scraper is advisory, as it will help you handle the sticky dough. If your dough is very sticky, oil is your friend and will help you work without having to add extra flour, which will mean your buns form a crust.

EASTER

Pasqua

While Sardinian Christmas is a fairly sober – almost sombre – affair, Easter is when festivities really come into their own.

'Of course, the birth of Christ is all very well,' says Monica, 'but his dying and coming back to life, well that's something to celebrate!'

The rest of the family nod in solemn approval. A natural love of the dramatic is somehow innately Italian, perhaps just innately human, and what could be more dramatic than dying on a cross, being buried in a stone tomb and then rising from the dead? What a story! Who can resist a happy ending?

Whether religiously observed or not, Easter is an important celebration in Italian households, and involves numerous specific foodstuffs. I have brought my beloved hot cross buns from England, and there is lamb (an English and Italian Easter tradition) and egg pies, too. Ricotta, eggs, greens, citrus, wild asparagus, all the best of the Sardinian spring is here to be cooked with. Tiny chickens and other decorated breads are made with extraordinary

dexterity and skill, spiked, frilled and curlicued, often with a boiled egg set within them. They are baked and then kept on mantlepieces or in linen drawers forever.

Holy week, or the week leading up to Easter, begins with Palm Sunday where here in Sardinia local palm sheaths are woven into extraordinary shapes, dried and displayed. Traditionally woven into sheaths, crosses and intricate plaits (braids), it is common to find them displayed in the corner of old houses. Easter Sunday is usually a family lunch, and then Little Easter, or *Pasquetta*, the day after, for celebrating and eating another long and large meal, usually with friends.

The quiet sobriety of Christmas is perhaps also due to the climate, which to most Sardinians is anathema. Easter, however, is more genteel in its meteorological offering, with temperatures that are *più simpatico*, meaning that spring walks can be enjoyed, and the sleepy summer suddenly feels not so very far away.

Preheat the oven to 180°C (350°F/gas 4).

To assemble, spread the mixture over the pastry base and use the back of a spoon to form five little nests or holes (make them fairly deep - the eggs need room) in which to place the remaining eggs. Crack an egg into each nest, draining off a little white if it is too abundant to fit in the nest.

Roll out the remaining two balls of dough to just under 1 mm (1/32 in) thick. Brush the overhanging edges of the pie base with a little water to help the lid stick and then place over the pastry lids (two layers, one over the other). Fold up all the way around the edge to form a neat pleat and seal the pie. Pierce the centre with a knife, then brush well with beaten egg.

Bake for 45–50 minutes until golden brown all over. Allow to cool slightly before serving, or serve completely cold. Either is good.

This pie is perfectly portable and great for picnics/packed lunches too. It keeps well in the refrigerator for a few days.

NETTLES

The humble stinging nettle is an ingredient that receives little attention, but merits more. Their prickly reputation should be no less off-putting than the spiky artichoke, their flavour as good as if not more interesting than spinach.

Ortiche, as the Italians call them, derive their name from the Latin *urere*, which means 'to burn' or 'sting'. They have been used for millenia to make fabrics and dyes and also for medicinal purposes. In the kitchen they can be blended into purées, soups, pestos and risottos, and are often drunk as tea. Until I had my own garden (garden being a generous description of the patch of scrub we call our own) I had never really thought of nettles as anything other than a nuisance. Then, once I began digging up the nettle patch monopolising the corner beneath the *nespole*, Monica stopped me and told me to make them into risotto.

There is something incredibly satisfying about using what is so often seen as a 'weed' as a principal ingredient, a sort of culinary championing of the underdog.

When gathering nettles it is important to wear gloves. Here with Monica, kitchen marigolds are traditional but any gardening gloves will do. Once you have picked them and plunged them into cold water they will no longer sting you. Their flavour is a little like spinach, but less iron-y and more peppery, a little like rocket (arugula). It has a nuttiness when cooked, and a gentle peppery undertone, an earthiness, grassiness and hint of cucumber skin. Just as nature would intend, in the kitchen they work brilliantly in bridging the brief divide between the bitter winter greens and the sweet spring leaves, peas and beans.

Creamy Nettle Risotto

Serves 4

a large (gloved) handful of back-garden/foraged nettles (young and tender ones work best)

bicarbonate of soda (baking soda), for soaking

2 tablespoons butter

1 tablespoon olive oil

½ white onion, diced

1 garlic clove, sliced

300 g (10½ oz/1⅓ cups) carnaroli rice

1 large glass of white wine or Vernaccia

800 ml (27 fl oz/3¼ cups) vegetable stock

100 ml (3½ fl oz/scant ½ cup) double (heavy) cream

3–4 tablespoons grated Parmesan cheese

salt and pepper

I think this is probably my favourite risotto recipe of all time. It would be hard to put words to the distinct flavour of nettles, but they are vaguely like borage, and a little like spinach, though with less of an iron flavour about them and a slight peppery note too. You'll know the scent once they're sweating in the pan, because it smells just like walking through the undergrowth and squashing them underfoot.

Almost everyone has access to a patch of nettles, growing wild and unwelcome as they do, and this recipe will make you see them differently, I hope. They work incredibly well in risotto, and this is one of my mother-in-law Monica's signature recipes. Every February she goes out scouring for nettles in her marigolds, comes back, soaks them in bicarb (one never knows where the cats have been) and then makes this. The cream, though very rarely used in Sardinia (and not often used in risotto), is a very welcome touch here.

Soak the nettles in lots of cold water with some bicarbonate of soda, then pick the leaves away from the stems. Discard the stems.

Heat the butter and oil in a saucepan over a low heat and soften the onion and garlic. Once translucent, add the rice and continue cooking for a few minutes, stirring. Now add the nettles, roughly chopped if the leaves are large (you can do this with scissors straight into the pan), otherwise toss them in whole. Allow them to soften and sweat a little and then add the wine. Simmer for a few minutes before adding the first ladleful of stock and stirring until it has been absorbed, then continuing ladle by ladle, stirring all the time, until the rice is *al dente*, which will take about 16 minutes.

Add the cream and cheese, and season to taste. Serve in shallow bowls.

Wild Green Gnudi and Sage Butter

Serves 4–6 (makes around 22 balls)

A charming name for a delicious thing, *gnudi* are really just nude *ravioli*: pillowy orbs of creamy ricotta filling stripped of their pasta jackets. They retain their shape instead with a delicate coating of *semola*, which forms a soft crust. Originally from Tuscany, but found in many parts of Italy, they are especially good when made with good-quality sheep's milk ricotta, something Sardinia has in abundance.

The real joy of *gnudi*, apart from their evocative name and their delicious flavour, is how simple they are to make. No faffing around making and rolling pasta dough, just a soft, ricotta-based mix, stirred roughly in a bowl, then rolled by hand and plopped in semolina. Some people add egg to bind the mix, but I generally keep it simple and use only ricotta, occasionally adding some greens and always nutmeg, a little lemon zest (not always traditional but I love it) and Parmesan.

Gnudi are also wonderfully versatile. In the winter I like to make mine pure and white. Served like this they resemble little snowballs sitting in a warm puddle of sage butter. In the spring I love to add some iron-rich greens to the mix, whether borage, nettles or spinach. In the summer I add some crushed fresh peas to make pale, pistachio-green gnudi. I almost always serve them with a simple sauce of melted butter and sage.

Be aware that these need to be made the day before you want to serve them, as they will firm up overnight in the refrigerator and their *semola* jackets will form properly, preventing any unwanted explosions as they cook in the boiling water.

A note on ricotta: if you can find real, fresh sheep's milk ricotta this should be firm enough to use as is. If you are using pasteurised tub ricotta (which is much wetter in consistency) you will need to line a sieve (fine mesh strainer) with muslin (cheesecloth) or paper towels and drain it for a couple of hours until it becomes more dense.

1 bunch of spinach/chard/
wild greens

good pinch of salt, plus extra
for the cooking water

500 g (1 lb 2 oz) fresh sheep's
milk ricotta

70 g (2½ oz) Parmesan, grated

grated zest of 1 small lemon

good pinch of grated nutmeg

around 700 g (1 lb 9 oz/
5¾ cups) *semola* (semolina),
to coat (you can sieve and reuse
this afterwards for making
pasta, etc.)

40 g (1½ oz) pecorino, grated,
to serve

For the sage butter

150 g (5 oz) butter

a few sage leaves

pinch of salt

First cook the greens in a large pan of salted water until tender (mere seconds), then drain them well. Allow to cool. When cool, use your hands to squeeze them well, removing any excess liquid. Chop them roughly with a knife (you can blitz them in a blender, if you prefer) and set aside.

Place the ricotta in a large bowl and add the freshly grated Parmesan, lemon zest, nutmeg and salt along with your chopped greens. Mix it all together, either with a fork or your hands. Taste for seasoning and adjust accordingly.

Pour a generous layer (2.5 cm/1 in deep) of fine semolina into a large tray (pan) with deep sides. With clean hands, take small walnut-size amounts of the mixture and roll them to form perfect spheres. Place them in the semolina and roll well so they that they have an even coating. Space the balls evenly over the tray and make sure each is well coated in semolina: you should not be able to see any white ricotta at all. Place in the refrigerator overnight, still on their bed of semolina.

The next day, turn the balls over and roll them briefly in your hands again to remove excess semolina. They should be nice and firm and evenly coated.

Bring a deep pan of well-salted water to the boil and gently drop in your *gnudi*. After a minute or two they should bob to the surface. Carefully lift them out with a slotted spoon and set aside.

Meanwhile, make your sauce. Melt the butter, then add the sage leaves and stir over a low heat. Add the salt and a splash of the *gnudi* cooking water and stir until you have a smooth sauce.

Serve the sage butter with the *gnudi*, with grated pecorino on top.

Butter and Honey Brioche Breakfast Buns

Makes 10

For the starter

20 g (¾ oz) fresh yeast
(or 10 g/½ oz dried yeast)

120 g (4 oz/⅓ cup) fragrant
honey

100 ml (3½ fl oz/
scant ½ cup) warm water
(at body temperature)

110 ml (3¾ fl oz/scant ½ cup)
milk (at body temperature)

220 g (8 oz/1¾ cups) strong
bread flour

For the final dough

130 g (4 oz) butter,
cubed and softened

400 g (14 oz/3⅓ cups) strong
bread flour

2 egg yolks

12 g (½ oz) salt

To finish

a little flavourless oil,
for greasing

milk, for brushing

honey, for glazing

Often the recipes that become my favourites are born by mistake. I was re-testing my Hot Cross Bun recipe on p.57 and was in a rush so left out the spices, citrus and raisins, just to test the simple enriched dough itself. I had some wonderful, fragrant spring honey from my friend, Luigi the Honey Man, and so added that instead of the sugar. The result was an instant hit. You can smell and taste the honey beautifully. Buns fit for Winnie The Pooh himself. And please don't be put off by the word brioche; they are incredibly easy.

Make the dough in the early evening, shape them before going to bed, put them in the refrigerator overnight to prove and then bake them straight away for breakfast. Waking up to this smell is something truly life-affirming.

For the starter, melt the yeast and honey in the warm water and milk, whisking well to dissolve, and then whisk in the flour. Leave, covered, for 1 hour.

Make sure the butter is at room temperature, otherwise it won't knead neatly into the dough (you can squeeze it in warm hands a bit to speed up this process – I always do this as I never remember to get it out of the refrigerator ahead of time).

Add the remaining ingredients for the final dough along with the starter to a stand mixer and mix until you have a smooth, even dough. If doing this by hand, this will look a shaggy mess at first, but revel in the kneading process as it comes together as a fairly neat and smooth dough. It will be a little tacky, but don't worry. Leave to rise overnight in the refrigerator, well covered, or at room temperature for 1–1½ hours until doubled in size.

Using a dough scraper and lightly oiling your (digital) scales, work surface and hands with a little flavourless oil, cut and shape the dough into balls of 100 g (3½ oz). Place the balls on a large baking tray (pan) lined with greaseproof paper an inch or so apart. Tuck them away somewhere warm and draught-free to keep them out of mischief. Let them rise for 1–1½ hours until doubled in size (this stage can also be done overnight in the refrigerator).

Preheat the oven to 180°C (350°F/gas 4).

Use a pastry brush to brush the buns evenly with milk. Bake in the oven for 14–16 minutes until golden brown. Remove from the oven and glaze, while still warm, with a pastry brush dipped in honey.

Eat as they are (these buns are good enough to be eaten alone) or split, toasted and topped with slabs of butter and extra honey.

Saffron, Honey and Blood Orange Ice Cream

Serves 6–8

4 egg yolks

100 g (3½ oz/scant ½ cup) sugar

250 ml (8½ fl oz/1 cup) whole milk

500 ml (17 fl oz/2 cups) double (heavy) cream

a good pinch of saffron threads (at least 8 stamens) or just under ½ teaspoon ground saffron

pared zest of 2 blood oranges (or 1 large regular orange)

120 g (4 oz/⅓ cup) honey (I use *millefiori*)

pinch of salt

This naturally has a wonderful chewy consistency due to the honey, meaning it stays lovely and soft and scoopable. The saffron is not too strong and provides a beautiful pale primrose colour.

You could use regular oranges if you prefer, and a delicate, floral honey (made in spring/early summer) works best here.

Make the custard the night before you want to churn and serve it to allow the flavours to develop.

Whisk the egg yolks with the sugar in a bowl.

Warm the milk, cream, saffron and pared zest in a small saucepan and bring just to a scald. Remove from the heat and pour over the egg yolk mixture, whisking well to mix.

Return the mixture to the pan and cook over a medium-low heat, whisking steadily all the time, until it is the consistency of double (heavy) cream and bubbles are beginning to form around the edge (this should take around 10 minutes at least). Whisk in the honey and salt and then decant into a clean container. Leave to cool before covering and placing in the refrigerator to mature overnight.

The next day, strain the mixture, pressing it well through a sieve (fine mesh strainer) to extract all the flavours from the saffron and orange zest.

Churn according to your ice-cream maker's instructions and serve.

Spring

Marinated Strawberries with Fresh Orange Blossoms

Serves 4–6

1–2 punnets of
good strawberries

1–2 tablespoons sugar

lemon juice

a handful of freshly picked
orange blossoms

The arrival of strawberries in Sardinia chimes with the first orange blossoms. The star-shaped white flowers known – rather wonderfully – as *zagara,* bloom against a background of darkly shining leaves, and the faint hum of bees becomes our background music once more. The flowers are purest white, their petals thick and succulent and easily snapped, the blossom itself highly perfumed, and when used in cooking it add its inimitable and exotic fragrance.

Orange blossom has long been used in perfumes and baking, particularly in the Middle East, and with the inheritance of certain sweet traditions that were brought by the Arabs first to Sicily and then to Sardinia it is a flavour that crops up in some *dolci* here, too. Associated with joy, good fortune and also supposedly an aphrodisiac, the scent is one I adore, and here it marries beautifully with fresh spring strawberries.

If you can't get hold of fresh orange blossoms, use a few drops of good orange blossom water.

I often serve this with a lemon semifreddo, or with a slice of simple sponge and some softly whipped cream. They also pair beautifully with ice cream.

Wash, hull and halve the strawberries, then place them in a bowl. Sprinkle over a spoonful or two of sugar and squeeze over some fresh lemon juice. Add the blossoms, stir gently and cover with a dish towel. Allow the strawberries to macerate until they begin to release their beautiful juice and then serve as you see fit.

Strawberry Tiramisù

Serves 6–8

3 eggs, separated

150 g (5 oz/⅔ cup) sugar

a scrape of vanilla seeds or
a drop of vanilla extract
(optional)

500 g (1 lb 2 oz) strawberries,
plus extra to serve

juice of 1 orange

juice of 1 lemon, plus a little
zest to serve

1 glass of Moscato
(or sweet wine)

500 g (1 lb 2 oz) mascarpone

26–30 savoiardi biscuits

mint sprigs, to serve (optional)

This is an homage to both trifle and tiramisù, and an ode to late spring/early summer. Lighter and also more child-friendly, it makes a wonderful picnic addition or birthday pudding. If you prefer to keep it non-alcoholic just use the fresh fruit juice to dip the savoiardi in.

If you like, you can make it in a 20 cm (8 in) cake tin (pan) and chill it overnight, in which case it will come out nicely birthday-cake like, once you have loosened around the edges with a hot knife.

Choose a container to suit your wishes. You can make this in a trifle bowl to serve in scoops, in individual glasses, or in a gratin dish to serve in squares (or scoops).

Whisk the egg yolks with 100 g (3½ oz/scant ½ cup) of the sugar and the vanilla (if using) until thick and mousse-like.

Wash, hull and halve the strawberries. Marinate them in the remaining sugar and the citrus juices plus the glass of Moscato. Set aside for 10 minutes while you finish the cream.

Add the mascarpone to the yolks and continue whisking until you have a smooth, pale-primrose cream.

In a separate bowl, whisk the egg whites until you have soft peaks. Fold the whites into the mascarpone mixture and mix gently until smooth.

Delicately dampen and dunk the savoiardi biscuits into the (now abundant) liquid from the strawberries and then begin layering. Start with a layer of soaked biscuits, then decorate with halved strawberries, then a layer of the cream. Repeat.

Place in the refrigerator to firm up (if you want to serve in neat slices) or serve as is, messily. Top with extra strawberries, lemon zest, mint sprigs, or as you see fit.

Strawberry, Lemon and Ricotta Almond Layer Cake for a Birthday

Serves 8–10

For the cake

100 g (3½ oz) butter, melted then cooled, plus extra for greasing

3 eggs

150 g (5 oz/⅔ cup) sugar

170 g (6 oz/1⅔ cups) ground almonds

70 g (2½ oz/generous ½ cup) plain (all-purpose) flour

pinch of salt

finely grated zest of 1 lemon

For the filling

500 g (1lb 2 oz) ricotta (see Note)

150 g (5 oz/⅔ cup) sugar

200 ml (7 fl oz/scant 1 cup) double (heavy) cream

1 teaspoon vanilla bean paste/ a scrape of the seeds from a pod

finely grated zest of 1 small lemon

For the strawberries

about 150g (5 oz) strawberries (2 small punnets or 1 large)

lemon juice and a little sugar, to macerate

To finish

icing (confectioners') sugar

edible flowers or rose petals

strawberries

This is based on something I saw once on a TV cooking programme as a child and then begged my mother to recreate. While I have experimented in the past with adding other flavours, there really is no better combination than strawberries and cream, and here ricotta forms a wonderfully rich and almost grassy foil to the fresh, raindrops-and-roses sweetness of strawberries. The cut berries, neatly lined up to expose their beautiful insides, are visually stunning. It is fancy without being fiddly, and beautifully, ethereally creamy and elegant to eat. It does, however, need to be made in advance if you want it to set up properly in the refrigerator overnight, but this is often a good thing and means you have a cake ready-made to take to a party. I make the same cake with poached pears in the autumn (in which case, exchange the almonds in the sponge for walnuts) and with figs in late summer (use hazelnuts). It is adaptable, impressive and delicious.

Preheat the oven to 170°C (325°F/gas 3). Grease and line the base and sides of a 23 cm (9 in) springform cake tin (pan) with baking paper.

Beat the eggs and sugar until pale, fluffy and mousse-like. Fold the almonds through the whisked eggs along with the flour and salt, then fold in the cooled melted butter and the lemon zest.

Pour the batter into the prepared tin and bake for 20–30 minutes until risen and golden. Set aside to cool.

Once cool, cut in half, using either a long carving knife or a piece of cotton thread. Place a half in the base of the (now clean) tin. You will build the cake in this and then release it to serve.

To make the filling, whisk the ricotta with the sugar until smooth. Add the cream and whisk again until thick, then fold in the vanilla and lemon zest. Place in the refrigerator to chill.

Hull the strawberries and cut them in half. Macerate with a light sprinkle of lemon juice and sugar.

Arrange the berries in an even layer over the base of the sponge, placing the outermost ring upright with cut-sides facing out, touching the sides of the cake tin. Spread over the cream filling. Place the second half of the sponge on top, then chill for 1–2 hours, or overnight.

Gently release the tin, running a knife carefully around the edges to ease the cake out, and smooth the sides with a palette knife if they smudge slightly. Sprinkle with icing sugar, decorate with flowers/rose petals and strawberries, then serve with aplomb.

NOTE: This cake needs a good, stiff ricotta so that the filling stays solid enough to support the structure. If you buy supermarket tubs of ricotta (often more liquid), let it drain for an hour or two (or overnight) in a sieve (fine strainer) lined with paper towels or muslin (cheesecloth) over a bowl.

SUMMER

Estate

Time was Away

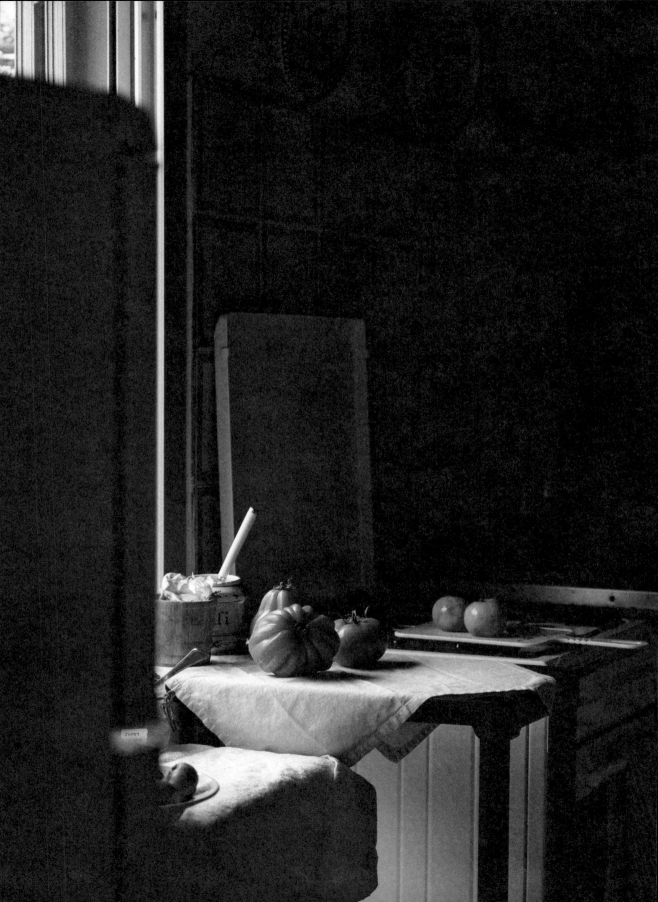

And so comes *L'estate*, with its sound like the gentle hiss of a beer bottle opening, or a whispering breeze in the Eucalyptus.

June is a dream, with flowers still full and the mornings still cool. We eat every meal outside; cold ricotta and hot coffee for breakfast with fresh apricots. The grain ripens, the wild poppies sway in the breeze, *campagna* begins to turn golden. Time takes on a different quality, the days stretch like a cat and the hours move stickily, drowning in honey.

Now is the time of the sacred Sardinian *secondo pomeriggio* (second afternoon). After lunch, and then the obligatory *pisolino* (even the most stoical of non-postprandial sleepers give in to Summer somnolence) there is an entire other afternoon, ready for the taking. The worst of the heat is over and from 4pm until sunset at 9pm the world is at your disposal. These are the hours for salty-sweet aperitivos or sitting in shuttered rooms eating cold slices of melon from the cold blade of a kitchen knife. I look at the lace curtain blowing in the slightest breeze, remember all my single summer English afternoons and smile.

The summer begins with cherries and ends with figs; in between there are apricots, peaches, melons - melons that never end. The white-fleshed toad-skinned melon of our region, the sweetest of all and the best to pair with prosciutto, grows like a weed during the driest months. To bite into it is to witness the true miracle of fruit, as it drips with juice. The *ortofruttas* (greengrocers) groan under the melons, the floor littered with them like footballs at a school gym. There are peaches from science fiction, so swollen that they solicit involuntarily sounds; cherries that shine as if buffed individually and burst when you bite into them. Swathes of fruit, crates of it: ripe today, bruised and fly-flecked tomorrow. Fruit to be eaten over the sink, face rinsed under the tap afterwards. Grapes continue to gather their sugars quietly, waiting until their time comes. We wake at dawn to *prendere il fresco* (take the cool), breathing in great gulps of it like medicine. The village moves its chatter outdoors,

setting up chairs on the pavement at dusk, staying out until the early hours, surrounded by squealing children, twitching cats and dozing dogs.

If the Maestrale is blowing, it is bearable (just) to eat outside. We take the dog to the beach and swim at sunset just as the sun sinks in a flamingo sky and the mosquitoes rise from the ground with a communal whine. The nights are sacred: we fling open all the shutters and sometimes a caress of cold air licks your foot, poking out of the single sheet under which you sleep, and it feels delicious.

July in Sardinia: it hasn't rained properly for nearly three months now, and each morning we wake to a sapphire sky – not a cloud in sight. The hedgerows are gold, the ground dry. The only green things left are the pale silver-sage of olive trees, as unshakable and old as time itself; people's pampered garden plants, watered every day at dawn and dusk in the dusty heat; and then the vines. The vines remain a glowing lush green as the ground around them dries to dust, and the once-proud weeds that grow between them wither and wilt in the sun.

'Do you water them?' I ask, innocently.

'Never,' scowls Mauro. Watering the vines changes everything, it ruins the wine. The vines must become strong, plant their roots deep and learn to cope on their own without us giving them water. Watering dilutes the wine and makes the vines weaker, dependent. They're made stronger by hardship. He winks.

Lorenzo flings open the windows one late July morning and tests the air, great nose twitching.

'Like a hairdryer,' he says, and closes it again.

Our clammy outdoor lunches are punctuated by the 'plops' of falling figs. Sleep is but a memory now; the insipid whine of a mosquito our lullaby as we lie awake and dream of air-conditioning. There are tomatoes in everything. We are leading up to the celebration of peak summer, the heathen holiday of Ferragosto on the 15 August, when you eat in groups outside, everyone sweating gently, the humidity at its most acute. And then at last it breaks and rains, and you know the worst is over.

Orange Blossom and Honey Amaretti

Makes 30 or so (good to freeze, or halve the recipe)

500 g (1 lb 2 oz/
3 generous cups) blanched
almonds, finely ground
(or 5 cups ground almonds)

240 g (8½ oz/generous 1 cup)
sugar

finely grated zest of
1 large orange

2 tablespoons honey (of your
choice – I use a citrus honey)

2 teaspoons orange
blossom water

a pinch of salt

100 g (3½ oz) egg whites

To decorate

nibbed, flaked (slivered) or
whole almonds

icing (confectioners') sugar

A twist on a classic, these are lovely and soft and chewy and wonderfully perfumed. The honey makes them extra sticky/chewy, and they go very well alongside aged Vernaccia/sherry or similar, or with a black coffee. They are good as Christmas gifts, too. The key to these, as with all amaretti, is not overcooking them and thus making sure they are extra soft and gooey in the centre. I add a pinch of salt to these as it works well to counteract the honey.

Preheat the oven to 180°C (350°F/gas 4) and line a large baking sheet with baking paper.

Place the ground almonds with the sugar in a large bowl. Add the orange zest, honey, orange blossom water, salt and egg whites, and mix with your hands to form an even, soft paste. It will feel just sticky, but not impossible to handle. Roll the paste into evenly sized pieces (about the size of an apricot) in your hands (dampen them if you like to make it easier). Place them on the sheet an inch or so apart from each other. Press them down slightly with your (damp) hands to form discs and decorate with either nibbed almonds, flaked almonds or simply with a single whole almond in the centre.

Bake for around 12-15 minutes until just golden but still soft-centred. Taste one to check, but don't burn your tongue. Remove and allow to cool either on the baking sheet or on a wire rack before dusting with icing sugar and eating.

Monica's Mezzalune alle Mandorle

Makes 16

300 g (10½ oz/3 cups) ground almonds

200 g (7 oz/scant 1 cup) sugar

zest of 1 lemon

2 eggs

dried fruit of your choice (most often raisins, or sour cherries or pieces of fig)

100 g (3½ oz/generous 1 cup) flaked (slivered) almonds (or other chopped nuts of your choice)

icing (confectioners') sugar (optional)

Monica doesn't have time for recipes. She makes things differently every time. Anyway, she says, she stole the recipe for these *mezzalune* (half-moons) from a magazine. The originals have cornflakes in them, which is a surprisingly effective addition.

She reminds me of two things, which I try to keep in mind always when cooking and when writing for other people to cook. Firstly, that no one 'owns' recipes, that we all assimilate them into our lives and our repertoires, adjusting and amending as we see fit and as situations and ingredients permit; and secondly that recipes are just a guideline but real life rarely follows guidelines, or sticks to plans or programmes, much as we would like it to.

Monica makes her *mezzalune* brusquely with whatever she has to hand, sticking to the basic formula and each time they turn out different. Sometimes she hits upon a winner (sneaking a little slice of fig inside) and sometimes she forgets about them and they burn to a black and bitterly smoking eclipse. Such is life.

Whatever way you choose to make yours, you will not be able to deny their adaptability and how forgiving they are to throw together. The base biscuit mix is almost identical to a classic *amaretti* recipe but they differ in the inclusion of whole egg (classic *amaretti* use only egg whites), which makes them richer. These are a little more homely and humble and lovable than the sophisticated *amaretti*, but retain that beguiling interior chewiness that is so satisfying.

Preheat the oven to 180°C (350°F/gas 4) and line a large baking sheet with baking paper.

Mix the ground almonds with the sugar, lemon zest and eggs until you have a paste. Using your hands, make half-moon shapes and press your chosen fruit, whether fresh or dried, into their centres. Dunk the tops of the cookies in the nuts to coat and place them on the lined baking sheet, spaced evenly apart.

Bake for around 10–12 minutes until just golden but still squidgy inside. Leave to cool on the tray or on a wire rack, then dust with icing sugar.

Variation

To make full-moons instead you can shape these as rounds. Make a little indent in the centre and then stick in your fig/cherry or a blob of your favourite jam.

Peeled Peaches with Prosciutto, Burrata and Basil

Serves 2

3 ripe peaches, yellow and white are good

1 large ball of burrata

salt, to taste

4 slices of prosciutto

a handful of basil leaves

extra virgin olive oil, for drizzling

A classic and cooling combination, elevated by peeling the peaches, which is a chore I adore. Plunging a heavy peach into boiling water for a few seconds and then lifting it out to gently rub away its papery skin is a sensual experience no summer should be without; along with eating seafood spaghetti by the sea and biting into a fig in a sunbeam.

The intense and explosive creaminess of burrata means that it pairs exquisitely with fruit, but you could replace it with a good mozzarella, which is also mild and creamy enough to work here. The prosciutto adds salt, the basil scent and summer musk. A perfect combination.

Bring a small pan of water to the boil. Remove it from the heat and gently drop in the peaches. Leave them for 10 seconds or so, then remove them with a spoon. Peel the skins away and discard. Slice them in half, then remove the stones.

Tear the burrata in two. Place a half on each plate and sprinkle with salt. Arrange the ham and peaches around the burrata, tear the basil leaves over and drizzle with oil.

Eat, with bread.

White Peach, Courgette and Pine Nut Salad

Serves 4

4 small courgettes (zucchini)

3–4 white peaches (or use nectarines if you can't find white peaches)

salt, to taste

zest and juice of 1 lemon

extra virgin olive oil, for drizzling

40 g (¾ oz/¼ cup) pine nuts

chopped fresh herbs, to serve (mint and parsley; or tarragon; or chervil; or basil would also be delicious)

I made this salad based upon a principle that I seem to repeat continuously; whether in my head or out loud to anyone listening: *things that grow together, go together*. Little pale green courgettes (zucchini), the colour of peeled cucumbers, crop at the same time as fairytale white peaches. Cutting into a white peach is like slicing open the most perfect water lily – the colours (ivory and purest fuschia) magically vivid.

Courgettes are undervalued raw. They work brilliantly in salads; sliced thinly and dressed simply they become nutty and lemony, and match perfectly with the fruit. The pine nuts provide a welcome savoury richness and some extra texture. You can add some cheese to this if you wish (burrata, mozzarella and a young pecorino or goats' cheese would all work well), but otherwise this is a simple, delicious and summery salad that relies on the fresh flavours of the individual ingredients.

It is very good served as a starter, or alongside creamy cheeses, or with some prosciutto. If you want to bulk out the salad, a large handful of rocket (arugula) leaves would also be good.

Finely slice the courgettes (you can peel them into ribbons or use a mandoline, based on preference) and the peaches. Lay them on a platter, sprinkle over some salt and the lemon zest, then squeeze over the lemon juice and drizzle over some olive oil.

Briefly toast the pine nuts in a saucepan over a low heat or place them in a 170°C (325°F/gas 3) oven for a few minutes until golden. Scatter them over the salad and finish with some freshly chopped herbs.

White Peach, Blackberry and Roasted Almond Pavlova

Serves 8–10

For the meringue

80 g (3 oz/½ cup) whole almonds (blanched or unblanched according to preference)

5 egg whites

a pinch of salt

250 g (9 oz/generous 1 cup) sugar

For the filling

250 g (9 oz) ricotta (tub ricotta is fine)

100 ml (3½ fl oz/scant ½ cup) double (heavy) cream

finely grated zest of 1 lemon

2 tablespoons icing (confectioners') sugar

To finish

3 white peaches

lemon juice

1 tablespoon sugar (optional, if the peaches are sour)

a handful of blackberries

a few lemon verbena leaves

I remember my very first white peach. I was on holiday in France as a child. Its heart and stone were a surreal shade of scarlet, the scent and flavour something that seemed to belong more to a mythical realm of flowers and fairies than that of the faded black leather of our battered old Volvo. We ate them in the car, in a heavy heat humming with the music of crickets, and I never forgot them.

In my local *ortofrutta* I find them again, their scent giving them away before I see them. Aside from eating them, I wanted to make a pudding that showcased their raw pink-and-white beauty, that reminds me of almond blossom. The same colour palette. I put them atop a pavlova, and in homage to the blossom they resemble, I added some roasted almonds to the meringue mix. Some blackberries made their way in there, too. And a few verbena leaves. You could use mint leaves instead. The ricotta cream provides a lovely light and not overly sweet topping.

Preheat the oven to 170°C (325°F/gas 3).

Scatter the almonds on a baking tray (pan) and place them in the oven. Roast for 11 minutes or so until just brown and beginning to smell wonderfully toasty. Remove and decrease the oven temperature to 140°C (275°F/gas 1).

Meanwhile, whisk the egg whites and pinch of salt in a clean bowl until stiff peaks form. Add the sugar, a spoonful at a time, whisking well after each addition. Continue whisking until you have stiff peaks once more.

Roughly chop or blitz the almonds and scatter around two-thirds of them into the meringue mixture, folding them through with a metal spoon.

Line a large flat baking sheet with baking paper and scoop the meringue onto the centre, smudging it with the back of a spoon into a rough circle. Scatter over the remaining almond pieces and place in the oven. Cook for about 1 hour 10 minutes until crisp, then turn off the oven and allow the meringue to cool inside as the oven cools down.

Remove after 30 minutes or so (although you can also leave it overnight), then allow to cool completely on the side before filling.

For the filling, whip the ricotta and cream together with the lemon zest and icing sugar until you have soft peaks. Spread over the centre of the meringue.

Slice the peaches and toss in the lemon juice and sugar (if using), then scatter them over the cream and sprinkle over the blackberries. Decorate with lemon verbena leaves, or as you see fit. Serve immediately.

Lorenzo's Aubergines

Serves 4 as an antipasti

3 large aubergines (eggplant)
(the Violetta variety
are the best)

sea salt

1 garlic clove, finely sliced

120 ml (4 fl oz/½ cup) good
extra virgin olive oil

a handful of fresh parsley,
roughly chopped

This is a classic antipasto in Sardinia, ubiquitous at any gathering or event, and it remains one of my favourites. The knack is to cook the aubergines (eggplant) near perfectly, a job I always allocate to the careful purist that is Lorenzo, who when given such a task executes it with the precision of a surgeon. Once cooked properly, the smoky sweetness of the aubergine becomes wonderfully pronounced, and is contrasted against a punchy fresh garlic, parsley and grassy olive oil dressing. The recipe involves nothing complicated, just the simplest ingredients, but a little extra attention and care.

There are various common additions if desired, such as chopped fresh mint, a little vinegar (balsamic is good), dried chilli. Flakes of salty cheese are also very good, as is a drizzle of honey and some fresh cheese (like ricotta, burrata or mozzarella). I usually keep things pretty pure as the flavour of the aubergines here is so spectacular on its own, but feel free to add as you see fit. This is an infinitely portable dish and is often prepared in foil trays for outdoor lunches and for taking as a picnic. Just add a fresh crusty panino, ripped open and stuffed with these and you have the perfect lunch *al mare*; salty, sweet, and with a hot hit of garlic.

It is important to pay attention to the small details here, such as the heat of the pan (keeping it medium and consistent, so all the slices cook evenly) and the thickness of your slices. If you have a mandoline (or even more fortunate – a meat slicer) then you can slice them evenly and quickly. A large sharp knife is also fine, just take a little extra care.

Wash the aubergines, pat them dry, then slice them into rounds about 7 mm (⅜ in) thick.

Heat a griddle pan (or a heavy-based saucepan) and cook the aubergines (dry), turning them just once, until they take on a good even colour all over on both sides and their mushroomy white flesh becomes translucent and floppy. Do this in batches in a single layer. Once cooked, place them on a platter and sprinkle with a good pinch of sea salt. Continue until all of the slices are done.

Mix the garlic with the olive oil, add the chopped parsley and mix with a pinch more salt. Pour over the aubergines and allow to rest for a while before serving.

Rigatoni with Fried Aubergines, Tomatoes and Ricotta Salata

Serves 2

Italian food enthusiasts will recognise this as an interpretation of the beloved and well-known *pasta alla Norma* from Sicily. Originally from Catania and named after Bellini's opera, *Norma*, it earnt its unlikely name after the Sicilian writer, Nino Martoglio pronounced it a 'masterpiece' on a par with the opera itself.

Despite its indisputably Sicilian heritage, this is a pasta dish that I look forward to making in my Sardinian kitchen every year, and that has taken on a form all of its own, which I'm not sure would wash as truly traditional. Nevertheless it is a beloved favourite; the perfect edible embodiment of the adage, less is more, a phrase that so often typifies the *cucina povera* dishes that proliferate in regions such as Sicily and Sardinia.

Simple is not the same as easy; so often the simplest recipes are the hardest to get exactly right. However, this dish is very far from difficult to achieve, instead it just requires attention to detail, relying as it does on a handful of simple but robust ingredients: aubergines (eggplant), tomatoes, basil and cheese. The sauce should be exquisitely balanced, highlighting the silky, sweet and smoky aubergine and just undercutting it with the acidity and freshness of tomatoes – either fresh or tinned – making sure they don't overwhelm the aubergine, which should be of equal significance in the finished dish. Frying the aubergines first in plenty of olive oil is where flavour begins to happen. Fry them really well until caramelised on all sides – this is what gives you the smoky sweetness that is so essential. If you see any of the aubergine that is still grey-green, keep cooking. They should be completely soft, gleaming with oil and beautifully blistered with coffee-like colouring.

The ricotta salata is essential here as it gives the dish a whole new dimension, rather than adding the ubiquitous grated Parmesan or pecorino. Instead, the ricotta salata makes this dish somehow more suitably summery, adding a beautiful white snowdrift-like crest to the pan, and also a lighter, fresher, more citrussy and acidic flavour that works well against the richness and depth of the smoky aubergine and tomato.

Once you have mastered this you will want to make it again and again: it is one of those combinations that should never be forgotten or changed, a truly timeless masterpiece. I cut my aubergines into chunks (I have often seen it prepared with thin slices, but I like them left a little larger as they become juicer and meatier once cooked and collapsing). I also use not-traditional rigatoni, a good robust shape that holds its own against the slippery aubergine. You can use penne or spaghetti if you prefer. I sometimes use garlic instead of onion, either is good. A single clove halved and fried at the beginning in place of the onion works well. The other essential, for me, is Antonella tomatoes. Sardinians swear by them – they are the best and sweetest, grown without pesticides, hand-selected and bottled within 12 hours. The tins make excellent pen pots.

Recipe continues overleaf

Summer

114

1 medium aubergine (eggplant) (look for a nice pert one, which should feel heavy and firm – the Italian Violetta variety are very good)

6 tablespoons olive oil, or as needed

½ onion, sliced

a pinch of dried chilli (I rip off a little piece from a whole dried red chilli)

250 g (9 oz) fresh ripe tomatoes, roughly chopped, or use tinned

1 teaspoon sugar or honey (optional)

200 g (7 oz) rigatoni, penne or pasta of your choice

fresh basil leaves

50 g (2 oz) ricotta salata, grated

salt

Chop the aubergine into small chunks around the size of a walnut and sprinkle them with salt.

Heat about 5 tablespoons of the oil in a deep, heavy-based saucepan over a medium-low heat and begin to sauté the aubergine. Turn regularly, making sure they colour evenly all over. If they absorb all the oil you may need to add a glug or two more.

In a separate pan, heat the onion and chilli in the remaining tablespoon of olive oil until the onion just begins to soften. Add the tomatoes and partially cover, turning down to a simmer. Simmer until reduced by at least a third and the onion slices are soft. Taste for seasoning. If your tomatoes were a little sour, you can add a teaspoon or so of sugar or mild honey here.

Once the aubergines are soft and coloured all over, add them to the tomato sauce. Cook for a few more minutes and taste for seasoning, adding salt or sugar if necessary.

Boil your pasta in well-salted water until *al dente*. Drain and add to the pan of sauce with a splash of the cooking water. Toss and stir well for a minute or two until the whole lot is creamy and squelchy.

Serve scattered with lots of fresh torn basil and the grated ricotta salata.

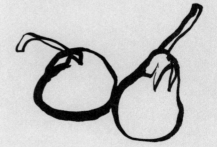

Peppers Piedmontese

Serves 2–4

2 large, ripe red peppers

a little salt

olive oil, for drizzling

2 garlic cloves, finely sliced

6 anchovy fillets, drained of their oil, sliced

4–6 medium ripe tomatoes (or use 8 or so small sweet ones, like datterini, if you prefer)

a handful of fresh basil leaves

A staple of my grandmother's, which she must have discovered via Elizabeth David's seminal *Italian Food*, published back in 1954 and still in print today. She gave me a beautiful edition of this book as my graduation present, painted all over with violet artichokes and garlic cloves, and it has been a constant companion ever since, and possibly even held sway over certain decisions of my adult life. Such is the great power of books and grandmothers.

She made this dish so often I have lost count of the number of times I have eaten it, always slightly different, depending on the ripeness of the peppers and tomatoes, her patience with peeling the garlic, how many anchovies she had curling in their tiny tin tucked away at the back of the refrigerator, how happy her indoor basil plant was, and the temperament of the Aga – if it was lively and full of vigour or slow and steady.

The queen of al fresco eating, it was she who booked concerts, day trips and gallery visits, took me to my first play and opera (I slept through the whole thing to her great chagrin), took us badger watching up on the hill behind her house by moonlight with deckchairs and hot sausages in a thermos. All such escapades would involve an obligatory picnic, and I, being as already obsessed by food as I was, would often forget the paintings and remember the pâté. These peppers are something she made often to bring and eat cold, alongside some good bread, or a slice of quiche, or her signature cheese sables, or egg and cress sandwiches, and it made truly perfect picnic food. It is true that the peppers are as good cold as they are warm (perhaps even better).

Extraordinarily simple and yet with a flavour as deep, sweet and savoury as any other dish I know, these deserve to become a staple in every household.

Depending on what peppers/tomatoes you get your hands on, this is a sort of rough guideline.

Preheat the oven to 180°C (350°F/gas 4).

Halve the peppers lengthways and remove their white innards and seeds. Place them in a snug baking dish, sprinkle lightly with salt and drizzle with olive oil. Scatter over the slices of garlic and the bits of anchovy. Slice the tomatoes in half and tuck them neatly into the pepper boats, cut-sides down. Drizzle with plentiful oil, sprinkle a touch more salt over and bake for about 45-60 minutes until just sagging and burnished.

Serve, garnished with the basil, at room temperature or cold.

Slow-cooked Chicken with Red Peppers, Anchovies and Basil

Serves 4–6

4–5 red (bell) peppers

1 tablespoon extra virgin olive oil

2 garlic cloves, halved

1 medium chicken, jointed (you can ask your butcher to do this for you), or 4 large skin-on, bone-in thighs

1–2 small sprigs of rosemary

5 anchovy fillets

a glass of white wine or Vernaccia

500 g (1 lb 2 oz) fresh ripe tomatoes (or tinned if you prefer)

a handful of fresh basil

salt, to taste

A simple, one-pot, late-summer chicken dish, which combines two of my favourite Italian classics into one: a most delicious Sardinian antipasti made of cold flame-roasted peppers, peeled and dressed with good olive oil, garlic and parsley/basil, and a Roman chicken dish with red (bell) peppers and pancetta. The pancetta in the Roman version adds a lovely savouriness to offset the sweetness of the peppers, and provides extra depth for a sometimes subtle chicken (there is nothing subtle about Sardinian chickens), but I have substituted it for anchovies here as I think they are even better with the sweet slipperiness of peppers and the occasional reticence of chicken meat.

Chargrilling the peppers separately over an open flame gives them a wonderful smokiness that is hard to beat, but if you are lacking in time or energy you can simply chop them up and add them to the pan at the same time as the tomatoes, or alternatively roast them in the oven beforehand and add them to the stew at the end.

Char the peppers over an open flame/your gas hob. Leave each part of them over the flame for a minute or two, turning them when you think of it, until they are well chargrilled all over. Place them in a bowl and cover with cling film (plastic wrap) for about 5 minutes. Once cool enough to handle, peel them of their charred skins (a quick rinse may be necessary) and remove their seeds and stalks too. Rip or cut into large strips.

Heat the oil in a wide, heavy-based saucepan/casserole with a lid over a medium-high heat. Add the garlic and cook for a minute or two until just beginning to take on colour. Add the chicken pieces to the pan (don't overcrowd the pan – do this in batches if needed), skin-side down, seasoning with a sprinkle of salt as you go. Brown the chicken pieces well, then turn them over and cook for a few minutes on the meaty side too, seasoning again with a sprinkle of salt. Once a good golden colour all over, remove the chicken from the pan and set aside.

Add the rosemary and anchovies to the pan and cook, stirring, until the anchovies have more or less melted. Add the wine and allow to simmer for a minute, then add the tomatoes, turn the heat to medium-low, add the chicken pieces back in, partially cover and simmer for around 45 minutes until the chicken is tender and just falling apart. Finally, add the peppers, simmer for a few minutes, then season and sprinkle with basil.

This is extremely good served at room temperature on hot summer evenings with a glass of strong, cold red wine and some crusty bread. Or you can serve it with some simply cooked fregola, orzo or couscous, if you like.

Fainè (Farinata)

Serves 3–4

200 g (7 oz/scant 1¾ cups)
chickpea flour (besan)

600 ml (20 fl oz/2½ cups) water

2 tablespooons extra virgin
olive oil, plus extra to serve

1 teaspoon sea salt, plus extra
to serve

3 tablespoons olive oil,
for cooking

Optional extras to serve

a little finely chopped onion
(nice young or spring onions/
scallions work well here)

small slices of salami known as
salsiccia sardo

In the north and south of Sardinia, both areas influenced by the influx of the Genovese, there exists a local version of the classic Ligurian speciality, *farinata*, known in Sardo as *fainè*. Around Sassari and Carloforte if you are lucky and it's the right season (autumn and occasionally spring) you can find this delicious chickpea pancake, cooked in flat round pans in a wood-fired oven once the pizzas are finished.

Like the classic farinata, fainè is a thin, olive-oil-enriched chickpea pancake with a crisp crust and a custardy middle. In Sardinia it is traditional to bake sliced *salsiccia* (the small cured pork salami) and onion into it, too. I have also heard of versions made with rosemary or lots of freshly cracked black pepper. The thin batter is allowed to rest before being cooked in a very hot oven in olive oil until burnished and crisp and then eaten hot, by the slice, much like pizza.

I heat the pan with the oil first, too, as I was taught to do with all things that you want to be extra crisp on the outside, like roast potatoes and Yorkshire pudding. As well as its beguiling texture, fainè has the added bonus of that unmistakable sweet, vegetal chickpea flavour, which works so well contrasted with salt and fat and that inimitable flavour of *fry*. The batter benefits from resting, but it is not essential, making this an incredibly easy thing to knock up in a hurry. I like to serve it instead of bread, with some 'picking bits' on the side, like a bit of cheese, cured meat or a juicy salad of some kind.

I cook mine in a 30 cm (12 in) pancake pan, but if you have a wide, round frying pan (skillet) that would also be good, just make sure it is ovenproof. Make your batter a few hours before you want to eat (you can also make it the night before and leave it to rest in the refrigerator).

Make the batter by pouring the water gently into a bowl with the flour and whisking continuously until smooth. Whisk in the extra virgin olive oil and salt, then set aside to rest covered with a dish towel.

When you want to cook, heat the oven to as high as it will go, about 250°C (500°F/gas 10).

Pour the olive oil into the base of your ovenproof frying pan (skillet) and place it in the oven to heat up. Once the oil in the pan is smoking hot, open the oven door and pour in the batter. Close the oven door and cook for 30-35 minutes until the top is burnished.

Serve immediately, sprinkled with extra sea salt and drizzled with your best olive oil. Add extra toppings if desired.

Some other ideas for toppings/sides

Gorgonzola and wilted radicchio (wilt with a little balsamic for sweetness) • Salami and olives • Gorgonzola and pear • Anchovies, tomatoes and ricotta • Ricotta and tomato • Basil, tomato and mozzarella • Anchovies, capers and mozzarella • Fried courgettes (zucchini) • Fried onions and stracchino • Grilled aubergines (eggplant) and pecorino

A GOOD SALAD

It has become perhaps banal to say there is more to a salad than sad lettuce and bad cucumber. I love a good plain green salad, well dressed, and with a fresh lettuce, simply tossed in good oil, lemon and salt. I adore a good fresh cucumber, peeled and sliced and tossed in the same way. The important thing is that both are flavoursome, in season, and preferably grown somewhere nearby. I also love to experiment and create salads that combine fruit, leaves, herbs, nuts, cheese, etc. There are no rules necessarily, only rough guidelines for when it comes to creating successful salads. These are:

Salt
There should always be a salty element in a salad, even if it's just some sea salt for seasoning. Other good salt contributors are anchovies, olives, capers (also acidity), bacon/pancetta, bottarga, cheeses.

Acid
The acidity of a salad is fundamental. Stronger salad components call for stronger acidity: red wine or balsamic vinegar in place of citrus. White wine (or Vernaccia) vinegar complements paler and more delicate flavours, as does lemon. Balsamic adds a touch of sweetness, which can work well with radicchio and aubergine (eggplant), among other things. I'd never dress fresh green lettuce in balsamic, for the two-fold reason that it changes the colour and is too strong. Lemon can be used to dress just about anything, but may need the boost of a wine vinegar if the flavours are forceful (in the case of anchovy or tuna salads, for example, I usually use a combination of lemon juice and red wine vinegar, as I do in my mayonnaise). Orange juice and other citrus provide a lovely light sweet-sour acidity perfect for fresh bright salads that contain fruit.

Texture
A good salad needs to have a pleasing texture, or combination of textures: crisp vegetables, crunchy nuts, crumbly or creamy cheese, etc.

Colour
A salad should look beautiful as well as tasting beautiful. At the risk of sounding pretentious, your white platter/plate is a blank canvas onto which you're applying colours/paint. I love composing salads using coloured ingredients as if I were using watercolours. Sunset pinks of peaches with pink-skin prosciutto, the burgundy of bitter radicchio and the dusky purple of figs.

Selection
Remember the old adage that 'things that grow together, go together' and you can't go too far wrong. Ingredients that are in season at the same time tend to have similar flavour profiles, and thus will generally pair well together.

Summer

Melon and Ginger Sorbet

Serves 4

400 g (14 oz) fresh ripe prepared melon flesh (deseeded and skinned)

2 lemons

160 g (5½ oz/scant ¾ cup) sugar

40 ml (1½ fl oz/3 tablespoons) water

a tiny pinch of salt

a walnut-sized nub of fresh ginger, peeled and grated

Based on a combination my granny used often as a starter (melon wedges sprinkled with powdered ginger) this is a refreshing and zingy sorbet that makes the most of both ingredients. Ginger works extremely well here, undercutting the somewhat ephemeral melon flavour with hot yellow fire and grounding its dewy sweetness in reality, rather than allowing it to float off into the gentle realm of meloninity. The lemon, too, keeps things nice and vigorous.

Light, fresh and perfectly balanced, this is a wonderful summer sorbet, and also works extremely well with/in cocktails/spritzes/summer drinks too, just use it in place of ice and add to prosecco, gin and soda, vodka and soda, rum, etc.

Here in Sardinia we are blessed with wonderful melons, the most common in our region are those with green skin and almost completely white flesh, which is what I often use here, but you can choose your favourite variety. My mum made it with a Galia melon, which is not renowned for being the most flavoursome, and she said it was still delicious. Canteloupe or Charentais give a lovely apricot-coloured sorbet.

Cut the prepared melon flesh into rough chunks and place in a blender. Squeeze over the juice of the lemons.

Make a simple sugar syrup. Add the sugar, water and pinch of salt to a small saucepan and place over a low heat. Add the grated ginger and a few strips of zest peeled from one of the lemons, then bring to a simmer and allow to bubble for a few minutes until it reaches a Vaseline-like, slimy consistency when you remove a little and touch it between thumb and forefinger.

Add the syrup (with the zest) to the blender with the melon and blend until smooth (you will sieve the mixture so it doesn't matter if the strips of zest don't break down completely).

Strain the whole mixture through a sieve (fine mesh strainer).

Churn in an ice-cream machine according to the manufacturer's instructions to the consistency of a sorbet, or place in a shallow container in the freezer and scrape with a fork every 20 minutes or so to create a refreshing granita.

Cherry, Pistachio, Lemon Frangipane and Fennel Cake

Serves 8–10

For poaching the cherries

200 g (7 oz) cherries, pitted

pared zest and juice of 1 lemon

3–4 tablespoons sugar

For the cake

200 g (7 oz) butter, softened, plus extra for greasing

a good pinch of salt

100 g (3½ oz/¾ cup) shelled pistachios

4 eggs

170 g (6 oz/¾ cup) sugar

zest and juice of 1 large lemon or 2 small

300 g (10½ oz/3 cups) ground almonds

2 teaspoons baking powder

2 tablespoons plain yoghurt

wild fennel flowers, to decorate

fresh cherries, to decorate (optional)

To glaze

1 tablespoon lemon juice

130 g (4 oz/1 cup) icing (confectioners') sugar

Here, cherries are poached briefly, then baked into a dense, nutty cake that is like a bakewell/frangipane tart without the faff of the pastry crust; just tinged green with pistachios and decorated with the wild fennel flowers I find in the hedgerow at this time of year.

Pistachios are precious and very expensive, so I use only a small amount here, giving the trusty almond the burden of providing the majority of the body of the cake. But the capricious pistachio adds its subtle smoky-butter nuance, and its pale grass-green tinge.

You can put the cherries in raw if you prefer (in which case skip the first step of the method), which I sometimes do if short of time, but I also like poaching them so you can have extra syrup, and they get even jammier once cooked in the cake.

Poach the cherries briefly in a splash of water with the lemon juice, a few strips of peeled zest and the sugar. Cook until soft, remove them with a spoon and set aside, then reduce the juice down to a syrupy consistency.

Preheat the oven to 180°C (350°F/gas 4). Grease and line a 23 cm (9 in) cake tin (pan) with baking paper.

Melt the butter either in a microwave or in a small saucepan over a gentle heat. Set aside to cool, then add the salt.

Blitz or finely chop the pistachios, reserving a few slivers to decorate the top of the cake, if you like. Chop them to a fine-ish crumb, but it is nice to have some pieces a little bigger, for texture too.

Beat the eggs with the sugar and lemon zest until combined, then add the lemon juice and melted butter, then the ground nuts, baking powder and finally the yoghurt. Don't worry if the mixture looks a little lumpy and curdled, it will settle down in the oven. Pour the batter into the prepared tin and plop in your poached cherries (some of their syrup, too, is fine).

Bake for 45-50 minutes until golden and firm. Allow to cool before removing from the tin.

Make a simple icing with the lemon juice and icing sugar. Glaze the cake, sprinkle with the reserved pistachio slivers and decorate with some fennel flowers and maybe a fresh cherry or two.

Serve with some of the cherry syrup and a blob of mascarpone as a pudding, or as it is with a coffee for breakfast or *merenda*. Any reserved cherry syrup can also be used in drinks/drizzled over yoghurt/porridge.

Fig, Gorgonzola and Fennel Flower Pizzette

Makes 4 pizza, serves 4–6

For the dough

200 g (7 oz/generous 1½ cups) *semola fine* (sometimes called semolata or semolina flour), plus extra for dusting

300 g (10½ oz/scant 2½ cups) '0' flour (manitoba or strong bread flour)

5 g (¼ oz) fresh yeast or 3 g (⅛ oz) dried yeast

10 g (½ oz) salt

350 g (12 oz/1½ cups) water, at room temperature

olive oil, for greasing and drizzling

For topping

8–10 fresh black figs, each cut into 6 pieces

300 g (10½ oz) gorgonzola dolce, cut into small pieces

a handful of wild fennel flowers

rocket (arugula) leaves (optional)

basil leaves (optional)

My favourite pizza of all, *bianco* (so without tomato sauce), but with sweet and jammy figs and the salty, creamy tang of gorgonzola. The wild fennel adds a lovely fragrant note and a splash of colour, but you could add a shaved fennel salad alongside if you prefer or if you can't find wild fennel. Leaves of peppery rocket (arugula), and strips of speck/prosciutto are also very welcome additions. Walnuts are delicious, too. You can make these as a sharing dish for a summer supper, or have one each.

I add *semola* to the dough, which makes it extra spongy and crisp, but if you find it hard to get hold of, use normal bread flour. Make the dough at around lunchtime to serve in the evening, giving it time for a nice long rise.

If adding rocket/basil/fennel or cured meat to your pizzette, add them after cooking rather than before, when the pizza is fresh out of the oven.

Mix the dough ingredients in a stand mixer (or by hand), kneading thoroughly until smooth and elastic (it is a fairly wet dough, so some slapping and folding on the surface will need the help of a dough scraper). You will need to mix it well and for at least 10–15 minutes for the *semola* to absorb the water (this is easiest if using a machine with a dough hook attachment).

Place the dough in a clean, lightly oiled bowl and cover with an oiled plastic bag. Leave to rise for 3–4 hours, giving the dough a couple of stretches and turns every now and then. Scoop your fingers into the sides of the bowl, pull out a flap of dough, then fold it back into the centre. Do this around the whole ball of dough (this helps to develop the gluten).

Once the dough is aerated and has doubled in size (after at least two stretches and folds), it is ready to use. Now either keep it in the refrigerator until you are ready to roll and bake it, or split it into four equal pieces and roll out immediately into small pizza-sized rounds, using extra *semola* or flour if necessary. Place on baking sheets.

Preheat the oven to 230°C (450°F/gas 8).

Dot the fig and gorgonzola pieces over the base of the rounds (along with any extra toppings of your choice), drizzle over some olive oil and bake in the oven for 10–15 minutes until golden and bubbling.

Serve immediately, sprinkled with the wild fennel flowers (and rocket/basil, if you wish) plus a drizzle of good oil.

Fig (Kind-of) Caprese

The Caprese salad is a cornerstone of the Italian kitchen, the classic mozzarella, tomato and basil mirroring the three colours of the Italian flag. Traditionally from Campania, where the best mozzarella is made, it has travelled all around Italy and can be one of the most soothing, lively, deliciously refreshing things to eat in Italian high summer.

Here I have played on the theme and used figs instead of tomatoes, their sweetness blending beautifully with the grassy milkiness of a good mozzarella, offset by the salty kick of a few small olives. The fragrant basil ties everything together nicely, as does some good, punchy olive oil. I like the green figs with red bellies the best for this salad, as they have a flavour that is a little grassier than the black variety.

Try to seek out a good mozzarella for this, if you can. I eat plenty of regular supermarket mozzarella, but for special occasions the real thing (made from buffalo milk) is worth finding.

This is more of a guide than a recipe …

2 or 3 figs per person

½ ball of mozzarella per person

a few small mixed olives

a few leaves of fresh basil

extra virgin olive oil

salt

Tear the figs in half (tearing produces infinitely more interesting pieces than neatly cutting) and break up the mozzarella into rough chunks. Arrange on your favourite salad plate, then scatter over the olives and basil leaves. Drizzle with some oil and sprinkle over a little salt, concentrating on the cheese rather than the figs.

Serve with some toasted focaccia drizzled with olive oil.

Ripe Figs and Gorgonzola

So many of my favourite things to eat are not recipes as such but simply good ingredients paired together. However, these combinations can also become the springboard that bounce us towards new and exciting recipes, or other, imaginative ways of combining these ingredients.

Take ripe figs and gorgonzola. A heavenly combination eaten on its own, but something that can morph into a number of delicious recipes, too. Fig and gorgonzola pizza is a favourite (see p.132). Fig and gorgonzola focaccia, fig and gorgonzola sandwiches, fig and gorgonzola salad (add some radicchio or endive), even pasta with figs and gorgonzola is good, either hot or cold.

Or you can just eat a ripe fig full of rain-grass-coconut-raspberry-jam flavour and a smudge of salty, creamy, tangy, oak-barrel-and-old-wine-cellar-flavoured gorgonzola and feel pretty happy about life.

Pork Chops with Figs and Buttered Balsamic Radicchio

Serves 2

2 tablespoons olive oil

2 pork chops
(around 250 g/9 oz each)

a generous glug of aged
Vernaccia, sherry or Marsala

3 figs, halved

2 tablespoons butter

1 head of radicchio, core
removed, sliced into wedges

2 tablespoons balsamic vinegar

salt and black pepper, to taste

Pig and fig, a match made in heaven. The butter and balsamic combination is a delicious and cunning way to take the edge off radicchio. I love its bitterness but know not everyone else does, and creamy butter and the musky grape-sweetness of balsamic do wonders for it. The perfect supper for the first cooler, late summer/beginning of autumn nights.

To make this more substantial, add some simple braised cannellini beans or bread or potatoes for starch. Braised greens would also be a good addition.

Heat the oil in a heavy-based griddle pan. Salt your chops well on both sides. When the pan is just beginning to smoke, add the chops and cook them until brown all over on both sides, making sure the middle is cooked through (you will probably have to turn the heat down to medium depending on your pan/stove). Set aside to rest for a moment and deglaze the pan with a generous glug of your chosen liquid, then add the figs and cook until reduced to a nice brown jus. Taste for seasoning and add more salt if necessary.

Meanwhile, in a heavy-based sauté pan, heat the butter until bubbling. Add the radicchio wedges and cook, allowing them to take on a little colour all over. Season well with salt and pepper, then add the balsamic vinegar and allow to bubble for a bit. Taste for seasoning and serve alongside the pork (it is nice if the radicchio is still a little raw in the middle – I love the contrast in textures, colours and flavours, so aim for caramelisation on the outside and some rawness in the middle).

THE SEASON OF FALLING FIGS

Eat more figs! **says** Mauro, *They won't be here for much longer.*

It is the season of figs – we go out in the field to pick more crates from Zio Mario's trees. There are little purple ones, which look like squirrel-sized Pied Piper bundle bags (known as a 'bindle', or in Sardo as *s'acaungiu* – the bundled lunch taken by *contadini* to *campagna*). These are *fichi neri*, and have paper-thin, dusky purple skins, berry-red interiors and a concentrated sweetness like hot blackberries and coconut. Then there are the biggest, known in Sardo as 'aubergine figs' – a large, elegant, tapered fruit, often as big as a lemon, blushed with shades of early autumn: sage green, camel and russet brown, and the faintest violet tinge. These have peach-pink interiors and taste of warm honey. Then there are the two 'white' figs, which in fact have grasshopper green skins; pert, squat, round and milky, their tight jackets burst open to reveal rose-pink interiors, juicier than the others, like ready-made jam, but fresh and grapey, with a flavour more grassy, like the first sweet, just-ripe strawberries, squashed. Finally,

there is my favourite of all, the one that offers least in terms of external appearance. Small, round and lime-green, when squeezed it breaks open to reveal a shocking scarlet interior, the colour and taste of raspberry jam. This is *sa mazza arrubia*, the red-bellied fig, and is rarer than the others, especially in our case as Zio Mario raids the tree early for his wife, Sofia; these are her favourites, too.

The figs are paired with proscuitto, with cheese, with ricotta, with bread and honey; boiled into jam, tucked into *panini e piadine*, baked onto pizza with gorgonzola and into tarts, pies and cakes. After each meal we eat ten or so as they are, washed and plonked in the centre of the table, bits of stalk and skin piled high on plates. The chickens enjoy the leftovers.

'Eat them now,' says Mauro, squeezing a fat fig between his fingers for the four-hundredth time this summer and inspecting its pink insides, 'You'll miss them when they're gone.'

Summer

Fig and Hazelnut Frangipane Farro Galette

Serves 8–10

Although it is not unusual for me to choose a recipe based purely on alliterative preferences, these are all things that genuinely go beautifully together, wordsmithery aside. Figs, farro, frangipane.

Frangipane has a wonderful (and seemingly messy) history. It sort of sounds like the beginning of a bad joke. There is a flower, a Frenchman, an Italian, and a female apostle of San Franscesco d'Assisi; a Latin phrase for good measure, too.

The Frangipani/Frangipane were a noble Roman family of the Middle Ages, their surname derived from the Latin phrase, *frangere panem*, which means to break bread. Some claim that the sweet derived its name from this, and most specifically from the late 17th-century marshal Marquis Muzio Frangipani, who invented an ingenious way of scenting his leather gloves with an almond-like perfume, a fashion that soon became popular enough to be copied not only by other glove-wearers, but cunning French pastry chefs who created a sweet with the same scent and name. The flower, too, derives its name from the fragrant Marquis.

Another story, equal in charm though perhaps inferior in probability, is that of Jacoba de Settesoli, a devout follower of St Francis, who fulfilled the dying wishes of the saint in bringing him his favourite 'almond sweet'. Her husband was a Frangipane, and it is possible that she gave her married name to the almond mixture. Like so many culinary stalwarts (my beloved béchamel included) both the French and the Italians can lay claim to this marvellous invention, and as is delightfully often the case, somewhere in the course of history, things got a little mixed up. All the better for us.

Whatever the fascinating origins of its name, frangipane as cooks now know it is an almond- or other nut-based mixture generally used to fill things, based around a cake-like mixture of butter, sugar and eggs. I usually use a simple ratio inherited from cheffing days of 1 egg for every 100 g (3½ oz) of everything else (butter, sugar and ground almonds). The hazelnuts make it feel wonderfully woody and autumnal, and work beautifully with the figs. The texture is bewitching: nubbly nuts suspended in soft sponge, the frequent crunch of seedy figs and the buttery flakiness and crumble of a good pastry blend to form a heady combination. It is also not overwhelmingly sweet (thanks to a relatively low sugar content), which allows the jamminess of the figs to truly shine and there's a whiff of a childhood fig roll buried in there somewhere.

You could also buy ready-made puff pastry and simply make the filling if you prefer, which cuts down the preparation time considerably.

Recipe continues overleaf

Summer

For the pastry

200 g (7 oz/1½ cups) white
farro (or spelt) flour, plus extra
for dusting

a generous pinch of salt

150 g (5 oz) very cold butter,
cubed

1 tablespoon Demerara sugar

1 teaspoon lemon juice

50 ml (1¾ fl oz/3 tablespoons)
iced water

For the frangipane filling

100 g (3½ oz/generous ⅔ cup)
whole hazelnuts (preferably
blanched)

100 g (3½ oz) butter,
slightly softened

100 g (3½ oz/scant ½ cup)
Demerara or light brown sugar

a generous pinch of salt

1 egg, at room temperature

5–6 figs, sliced into thin slices

To finish

1 egg, beaten

1 tablespoon Demerara sugar
(optional but adds crunch)

For the pastry, place the flour and salt in a large mixing bowl. Add the cubes of butter and toss them in the flour with your fingers, making sure that they are all coated. Begin to press them into flat discs in your fingers, tossing as you do so to make sure they stay coated in flour. Once all the cubes become flakes and are well distributed through the flour, add the sugar, lemon juice and water. Bring the dough together with your hands (if it still looks too dry and flaky add a touch more cold water). It is quite a rough dough, so do not aim for smooth, even and shiny, but it needs to come together in one clean piece with no dry bits at all. Pat it into a round, wrap in cling film (plastic wrap) and chill for at least 40 minutes in the refrigerator or freezer.

When ready to assemble the tart, roll the pastry out to a 3-4 mm (⅛ in) thickness (this is quite a rustic tart and the pastry is nice eaten relatively thick). Roll it directly onto a piece of baking paper, and if things begin to look sticky add a dusting of flour or place another piece of baking paper over the top and continue rolling. Aim for a rough round. Place back in the refrigerator while you make the filling.

Preheat the oven to 170°C (325°F/gas 3).

For the frangipane, scatter the hazelnuts over a baking sheet and roast in the oven for 10–13 minutes until they are just camel-coloured and smell delicious. Remove, allow to cool for a few minutes and then blitz them (or chop by hand) until you have a relatively fine, sandy rubble (it's nice to have a little texture here, with a few slightly larger pieces and the rest more sandy). Set aside.

Beat the butter, sugar and salt until pale and fluffy. Add the egg, a little at a time, beating all the time until incorporated. Finally, beat in the (cooled) ground hazelnuts. Chill for 20 minutes or so (you can also make this in advance and chill overnight, just allow it to soften up a little before using).

Turn the oven up to 190°C (375°F/gas 5).

Place your pastry disc (still on its baking paper) on a flat baking sheet and gently spread over the frangipane mixture, leaving a 5 cm (2 in) border. Lay the fig slices over the frangipane, pressing them in gently. Tuck the edges of the pastry disc in, one pleat at a time, to create a rough round.

Glaze the pastry borders with the beaten egg and sprinkle over the Demerara sugar, then bake in the oven for around 45 minutes until the pastry is dark golden and the fruit bubbling. You may have a little leakage around the side of the galette (especially if your pastry has a crack or two) but if you want to present it perfectly lift it off the sheet and neatly onto a plate. The caramelised leaky bit can be eaten as a chef's perk.

Serve warm or cold, with some mascarpone, cream or thick yoghurt.

This keeps well in the refrigerator for a few days.

Strawberry and Fig Leaf Jam

Makes enough for about 3 jars

650 g (1 lb 7 oz) strawberries

1 lemon

250 g (9 oz/generous 1 cup) sugar

4 fig leaves, washed and stalks removed, plus extra to decorate

This combination came about by happy accident, a tentative foray into food matchmaking, or playing culinary Cupid. In early May the fig tree began to perfume the garden with the warm scent of its leaves, which wafted over as I washed strawberries in the outdoor sink. I decided to try to pair the two ingredients, and this delicious jam is the result.

This jam has now become a favourite, and is a wonderful thing to give as a gift, as it is somewhat unexpected.

Note: I usually adjust the sugar slightly depending on how ripe the fruit is.

The night before you want to make your jam, wash, hull and halve the strawberries. Cut the lemon into six or so pieces and squeeze their juice over the strawberries (remove any pips), then throw the pieces into the bowl too. Add the sugar and the fig leaves torn into rough pieces. Stir, cover with a cloth and leave to macerate overnight in a cool place.

The next day, sterilise your jars (see p.169).

Remove the lemon pieces and fig leaves from the bowl and discard. Bring the strawberries and sugar to a simmer in a deep pan and cook for around 10–15 minutes, before testing to see if setting point is reached (dribble a little onto a cold saucer, wait for a few seconds, then push it with your finger; if wrinkles appear, your jam is ready).

Pour into the sterilised jars, add a fig leaf to each jar, then seal and store (or use in the cake on p.144).

Summer

143

Victorious Sponge with Cream and Strawberry Fig Leaf Jam

Makes 1 cake (serves 8–10)

250 g (9 oz) softened butter, plus extra melted for greasing

250 g (9 oz/generous 1 cup) sugar

finely grated zest of 1 lemon (optional)

a good pinch of salt

4 eggs, at room temperature

250 g (9 oz/2 cups) plain (all-purpose) or '00' flour

30 g (1 oz/¼ cup) potato flour

1 packet of *lievito per dolci* (with or without vanilla flavouring) or 3 teaspoons baking powder and some vanilla extract

4 tablespoons milk

To finish

1 medium jar of Strawberry Fig Leaf Jam (see p.143), or your favourite jam

250 ml (8½ fl oz/1 cup) double (heavy) cream, softly whipped

icing (confectioners') sugar, sifted, for dusting

fresh strawberries or other fresh fruit/flowers of your choice

I never know whether May is really spring or summer. It's a cusp month, a bit of both and yet its own time too, and that's why I love it; I am always attracted to things that defy easy definition. (September, my other favourite month is similar; sort of autumn and yet still a little sticky with summer.) The first flopping roses appear, there are finally outdoor breakfasts (or teas) with cake on the table and that inimitable smell of warm jam and cream together.

This classic sponge, while undeniably English, is much appreciated by every Italian I have ever introduced it to. It has somewhat of a cult status in Italy, as the ubiquitous centrepiece of our famed 'English Tea'. The arrival of my birthday in May means afternoon tea, a tradition taken from my old home to my new one, now heartily adopted in Sardinia too. My mother-in-law is a complete convert, and serves tea in her garden complete with dainty china and tiny white-bread sandwiches.

While a classic Victoria needs little tampering with, I wanted to add some potato flour as a nod to many Italian cakes that use it to great effect; it ensures a more tender crumb. You can substitute it with cornflour (cornstarch) if you prefer, or omit. I sometimes fill the sponge with a combination of fresh fruit (strawberries, raspberries and blackberries are favourites), jam and cream, or sometimes just jam and cream – both are good. This cake will keep for a few days in a cool place, but is best eaten the day it is made, or the day after, for breakfast.

For this sponge it is important to have all the ingredients at room temperature, otherwise the mix will split.

Preheat the oven to 180°C (350°F/gas 4). Grease and line two 20 cm (8 in) shallow (sandwich) cake tins (pans) with melted butter and baking paper (or use a single deep cake pan if you don't have sandwich tins).

Beat the butter, sugar, lemon zest and salt until pale, soft and fluffy.

Break the eggs into a bowl and add them to the mixture a little at a time, beating well after each addition to make sure they are incorporated.

Weigh out the flours and add the raising agent, then add all at once to the mixing bowl and mix briefly until smooth. Add the milk and mix again for a few seconds.

Divide and smooth the batter out into the tin/s, then bake on the middle shelf of the oven for 25-30 minutes until golden and an inserted skewer comes out clean (if it is still undercooked in the middle, turn the oven down and continue cooking). Leave to cool for a few minutes before turning out onto a wire rack to cool completely.

If you have made a single sponge, cut it in half horizontally. Spread the jam over the bottom sponge, then spread over the whipped cream to form a billowy but even layer. Place the clean sponge on top and top with sifted icing sugar and strawberries or fresh fruit/flowers of your choice.

Plum and Wild Fennel Jam

Makes around 4 small jars

900 g (2 lb) plums (greengages, yellow plums or Victorias are all good options)

zest and juice of 1 large lemon

a few wild fennel flower heads (if you can't find the flowers you can use 1 teaspoon of fennel seeds but make sure they are fresh and green and citrussy rather than brown, toasty and smoky)

500 g (1 lb 2 oz/2 generous cups) sugar

Wild fennel is a symbolic plant of Sardinia. It grows like a weed and its development throughout the year provides a cook with some sort of edible reward whatever the season. The fresh green shoots that sprout from the ground in spring are sweet and grassy and can be used in salads or to flavour dressings, soups and marinades; they work like any other soft herb and can add an aniseedy lift to ricotta, ravioli, frittatas, pies and pulses. The flower heads bloom in late June and are heady and honey-like; the seeds that come later toasty with hints of caraway, lemon and liquorice. By mid-July this hardy plant is one of the only green things left jutting proudly out of the parched golden hedgerows. Their tall, pale green and statuesque silhouettes frosted with miniature yellow blossom are one of my favourite sights at dusk. Picking them among the vines one evening, I decided to put them into a plum jam, which adds an extra edge to a fruit that can sometimes need a little nudge. The supple, lazy-honey flavour of plums responds well to something so sharply fragrant.

I make all my jams now by marinating my fruit first before boiling, a trick I learnt from one of my favourite jam-makers, Anna. This way the fruit begins to break down of its own accord and you have to cook it less; effectively all you are then doing is reducing the liquid. It's a sort of cold pre-cooking and keeps the flavour of the fruit fresher.

Marinate the plums in the lemon zest, juice, fennel flowers (or seeds) and sugar for at least 1-2 hours before beginning (you can do this overnight in the refrigerator, if you prefer).

Bring everything to a simmer in a deep saucepan and cook at a gentle rolling boil for up to 50 minutes until setting point is just reached. (Keep a saucer in the refrigerator and dribble a little jam onto it, leave for 20 seconds and then push your finger through the puddle; if wrinkles appear, the jam will set.) At this point you can sieve (strain) the jam or pass it through a moulis to remove the pips, flowers, etc., but I often don't bother.

Pot in sterilised jars (see p.169) and store. This is very good on thick yoghurt, or served alongside aged pecorino.

Baked Ricotta Cheesecake with Raspberry and Rose

Serves 8–10

For the base

100 g (3½ oz) butter, plus extra for greasing

120 g (4 oz/1 cup) plain (all-purpose) flour

60 g (2 oz/¼ cup) sugar

40 g (1½ oz/½ cup) flaked (slivered) almonds

a good pinch of salt

For the filling

300 g (10½ oz/1¼ cups) cream cheese

500 g (1 lb 2 oz/ generous 2 cups) ricotta

250 g (9 oz/generous 1 cup) sugar

a pinch of salt

1 tablespoon cornflour (cornstarch)

zest and juice of 2 lemons

4 eggs

For the raspberry layer

150 g (5 oz) raspberries

juice of 1 lemon

80 g (3 oz/⅓ cup) sugar (add more if your raspberries are very sour)

2 teaspoons cornflour (cornstarch)

a few drops of rose essence (optional)

rose petals, to decorate (optional)

Using mostly ricotta means that this cheesecake is wonderfully light rather than overpowering, in that magical way ricotta has of making everything it is baked into a beguiling and contradictory combination of moist, fluffy, creamy, dense and light. Creating your own biscuit base also works brilliantly. I add some almonds for extra texture and nuttiness, and it is not too buttery but wonderfully crisp; Goldilocks-balanced. The raspberry topping is fresh and sharp, a quick jam/compôte lifted by a little rosy perfume.

Preheat the oven to 160°C (300°F/gas 2). Grease and line a 23 cm (9 in) loose-bottomed cake tin (pan) with baking paper.

Blitz the ingredients for the base together in a food processor until you have a fine crumb (or rub the butter in by hand as if making a crumble – the almonds will break up sufficiently between firm fingers). Using the back of a spoon, press this mixture over the base of the lined tin to form an even layer.

Bake for 30 minutes until golden. Remove and set aside to cool.

Meanwhile, make the filling. Blend the cream cheese, ricotta, sugar and salt, and blitz/whisk until smooth. Mix the cornflour with the lemon zest and juice and stir well to dissolve. Beat this into the cream mix, then beat in the eggs, one at a time, until smooth. Pour the filling over the baked base. It will look very loose, but don't worry, all is well.

Bake in the oven for 50 minutes, then turn off the oven, leave the door open and leave the cheesecake to cook gently in the residual heat for another 50 minutes.

Remove and allow to cool for at least 1 hour before serving.

For the raspberry layer, cook the raspberries over a low heat with the lemon juice and sugar for about 8-10 minutes until you have a loose jam. Remove from the heat, ladle off a spoonful of juice and add it to the cornflour. Stir well until the flour dissolves, then add it to the pan and stir over the heat for a minute or two (the cornflour makes the raspberry mixture thicken without you having to reduce it down and cook out all the fresh flavour of the raspberries). Remove from the heat, decant into a bowl and leave to cool.

Stir the rose essence into the raspberry mixture (if you like – it's also very good kept simply raspberry), then top your cooled cheesecake with it. Serve, with added rose petals if you wish.

Cherry and Mascarpone Custard Crostata with Olive Oil Pastry

Serves 8–10

For the pastry

1 whole egg plus 1 yolk

70 ml (2½ fl oz/5 tablespoons) olive oil

1 teaspoon salt

70 g (2½ oz/scant ⅓ cup) sugar

250 g (9 oz/2 cups) plain (all-purpose) flour

For the filling

3–4 tablespoons cherry jam (see Note)

3 eggs

300 g (10½ oz/scant 1½ cups) mascarpone

120 g (4 oz/generous ½ cup) sugar

2 teaspoons vanilla paste (or seeds scraped from a pod)

grated zest of 1 large lemon

30 g (1 oz/¼ cup) cornflour (cornstarch), sifted

180 g (6½ oz) fresh cherries, pitted (you can also use frozen/tinned cherries, if you wish)

It is a cruel irony that just when fruit in Sardinia is at its most abundant, practically begging you to bake it with heavy, purple-lidded eyes, the very last thing you want to do is turn on the oven and get to work pounding pastry and whisking eggs. However, this olive oil pastry dough is so easy to make and needs no resting, chilling, or blind-baking. With a mascarpone filling that requires no pre-cooking or whisking, this crostata is perfect for summer breakfast with a strong coffee: an instant, lazy, July-worthy tart that celebrates ripe cherries and suspends them in purple-stained, egg-yellow, velvety custard.

There is a whiff of clafoutis, a whisper of custard tart, a memory of Bakewell, a murmur of cheesecake. If eaten hot (which I love, too) it is more like a soufflé/clafoutis (serve with cold cream and extra poached cherries), the egg wobbling and sweet. If eaten cold it is firmly in the cheesecake camp, but it is better than cheesecake because it is wonderfully light as well as creamy and velvety, and avoids that cloying quality cheesecake so often has. A tart for every occasion, and so very forgiving. It keeps well for at least four or five days in the refrigerator.

Note: As this tart is designed to be no fuss and very quick I have given the option of spreading some ready-made jam onto the base. What I like to do, when I have a little more time, is to make a very quick jam myself by poaching 200 g (7 oz) cherries with a little lemon juice and a very little sugar, and then to spread this on the base (still warm is fine).

First make the pastry. Add the whole egg, yolk, oil, salt and sugar to a bowl and whisk. With a wooden spoon, stir in the flour until the mixture comes together as a smooth dough (at this point start using your hands to bring it together). You can now wrap the dough and chill it, if you like, or roll it out immediately (or put it in the freezer for future use).

Preheat the oven to 170°C (325°F/gas 3).

Roll out the pastry on a large sheet of greaseproof paper to fit a 23 cm (9 in) tart or pie tin (pan) - I use a crostata tin with sides at least 2.5 cm (1 in) deep. Use the paper to help you flip the pastry onto the tin and peel it away. Trim the edges. Alternatively, press the dough roughly into the tin with your fingers (I often do this). Spread the jam over the pastry (if using) and set aside.

Mix the eggs into the mascarpone, whisking, then add the sugar, vanilla, lemon zest and cornflour, whisking well until smooth. Pour into the pastry case and scatter over the cherries.

Bake in the oven for 40-50 minutes until golden and only just wobbling in the middle. Remove and serve hot, if you like, with cold pouring cream or allow to chill completely before serving in slices.

NON TI SCORDAR DI ME

Forget-me-nots

We sit around the table one Sunday eating food and talking about eating food.

Monica (Lorenzo's mum) plans the following Sunday's menu; there are guests coming, so she has pen, paper and plans.

'We'll have sliced tomatoes, as a side dish,' she says. 'They are always so good.'

'Of course not!' replies her husband Mauro, with that peculiar emphasis Sardinians reserve for matters of the table. 'We'll have whole tomatoes and each person can cut and salt his own, as is right and proper and good.'

An epiphany strikes Mauro mid-sentence, and he slowly turns to me with that faraway look I know of old; the soft, golden glimmer of nostalgia.

'Have you ever eaten a fresh tomato cut in half and then spread salt across it with your knife like you would spread butter?'

Pause for dramatic effect ...

'It is the best thing in the whole world.'

His eyes shine like blackberries.

'No,' I say, 'I don't think I have.'

He takes a plump plum tomato from a nearby bowl, its spidery stalk still attached, and slices it in half lengthways. He dips and lifts out a flat knife-side of sea salt and spreads it thinly across the wet surface of the tomato.

He offers it to me with the air of a priest presenting a communion wafer.

'Here, try it.'

There are flavours so resonant, so evocative and so familiar that they almost cease to be flavours and instead become sensations, so closely linked are they to memory, to a moment in time, to a hundred moments that have passed when you have eaten a sun-ripened tomato sprinkled with salt and felt the burst of its tight skin in your mouth, the cold, sharp, amber jelly of its seeds rush over your teeth and tasted on your tongue the honey sweetness of its red flesh.

Mauro watches as I eat the tomato half, and nods with approval.

'My father taught us to eat them like that. It's always the simplest things that stay with you.'

'And – in the end – the best things are always the simplest,' chimes Monica. Conjugal conciliation found in a cut tomato.

Cold Tomatoes Stuffed with Rice, Tuna, Basil and Capers

Serves 2–4

130 g (4 oz/⅔ cup) carnaroli/arborio rice

extra virgin olive oil

3–4 medium–large tomatoes

3 tablespoons mayonnaise (homemade [p.229] would be grand, but bought is fine)

100 g (3½ oz) tuna, drained

2 teaspoons capers

a few torn leaves of fresh basil, plus extra sprigs to garnish

a little finely chopped spring onion (scallion) (optional)

½ teaspoon red wine vinegar (optional)

salt, to taste

This is one of the most refreshing and retro things you will ever eat on a hot summer afternoon, and was introduced to me by Stefano Vellebona, a brilliant cook and connoisseur of Sardinian food. They were a speciality of his mother's, and I ate them one evening in Alghero when visiting him. I have made them every midsummer since and thought of him.

There are few foods that are genuinely good fridge-cold, but this is one of them, and they benefit, too, from sitting around a bit to let the flavours settle and subsequently sing. Make them the night before, if you like, then present the entire platter straight from refrigerator to table, and you have lunch done. A little focaccia and a green salad or some cured meats/cheese would be ample accompaniment.

The basil must be fresh and abundant, and the tuna preferably of good, flavourful quality (try to find chunks in jars of olive oil, which tends to be better). The tomatoes, too, should be sweet and juicy. A perky basil sprig is used to mimic the tomato leaves, if you wish to take the *trompe l'oeil* to full fruition.

Cook the rice in well-salted water until *al dente* (about 14 minutes, depending on your rice). Drain and season with some olive oil. Allow to cool.

Cut the tops off the tomatoes to make little hats, then scoop their fleshy insides out into a bowl. Squish these fleshy insides between your fingers to break them up. Depending on how juicy your tomatoes are, add about half of this fleshy mix to the rice, then add the mayo, tuna, capers, basil, and spring onion (if using), and mix well. Taste for seasoning and add some more salt and acidity if necessary. (If you have made your own mayo according to the recipe on p.229, it is unlikely you will need to season things up too much. If using bought mayo, I usually add a little extra vinegar and punchy olive oil, and salt, too.) It needs to be highly seasoned to counteract the cold sweet flesh of the tomatoes.

Fill the tomatoes until full, replace their hats, and chill in the refrigerator for at least 1-2 hours, or overnight.

Serve, with basil sprigs to mimic leaves.

Confit Tomatoes

Makes enough to fill 2 large kilner jars

I wish I was someone who planned ahead. My grandmother was a great planner, always making menus, a great advocate in 'staying on top of your groceries' and generally militant domestic management. Freezers were stocked, breadcrumbs bagged and labelled, Christmas puddings and cakes made dutifully every stir-up Sunday. In my defence, midsummer in Sardinia flouts any attempt at forward planning as even the keenest and cunningest are faced with fast-wilting produce (it drops before your very eyes) and a brain that has been replaced with a fat, yellow peach. There it sits, seeping sweet juice happily, but not of great practical use.

Enter confit tomatoes. When you have lots of tomatoes (which you will), you just cook them in this way, store in the refrigerator, then fold them through pasta sauce, toss into salads, tuck into focaccia, or top on pizza. They are endlessly useful and keep for up to a month. You can use whatever herbs you have growing/around. I like to add wild fennel (or fennel seeds) sometimes too.

100 ml (3½ fl oz/scant ½ cup) olive oil

2 teaspoons honey

2 teaspoons red wine/sherry vinegar

a large pinch or two of salt

700 g (1 lb 9 oz) small tomatoes (cherry or datterini)

2 garlic cloves, peeled

1 dried chilli, torn

a few sprigs of herbs of your choice (marjoram, rosemary or thyme are all good options)

Preheat the oven to 150°C (300°F/gas 2).

Mix the oil, honey, vinegar and salt together and whisk briefly. Place the tomatoes snugly in a deep baking dish. Pour over the liquid, add the garlic, chilli and the herb sprigs. Roast, uncovered, for around 1-1½ hours until the tomato skins are shrivelled and just burnished.

Store in jars in the refrigerator, covered with their oily juices.

Confit Tomato and Roast Almond Pesto

Serves 6–8 (makes 2 small jars)

This is a spin on the Sicilian classic *pesto Trapanese*, which rather than being based around pine nuts employs almonds and tomatoes, too. I have seen versions of it with sun-dried tomatoes, some with raw almonds, some with raw, peeled tomatoes. Here I use confit tomatoes to get a really deep, smoky flavour, and the almonds also feel the kiss of the oven.

If you wanted to make this a little fancier, you could serve it with some good grilled prawns (shrimp), which is a delicious combination Luca used to make. It is very versatile and can also be used as a dressing for roast vegetables, or tossed through boiled potatoes, or served on some bruschetta with a little ricotta and fresh basil. Make a large batch and keep it in the refrigerator.

90 g (3¼ oz/generous ½ cup) almonds (either skin-on or blanched is fine)

200 g (7 oz) Confit Tomatoes (see left)

60 g (2 oz) aged pecorino, grated or crumbled

1 garlic clove, peeled

a handful of fresh basil

100 ml (3½ fl oz/scant ½ cup) olive oil (including some from your confit toms, if you like)

salt, to taste

Preheat the oven to 170°C (325°F/gas 3).

Toast the almonds on a baking tray (pan) in the oven for 12 minutes or so, until just smelling good and with a little colour. Remove and allow to cool.

Now, you can choose to keep this chunky and chop/mix everything by hand, or in a pestle and mortar, or you can opt for a smoother sauce and throw it all in a blender and blitz until it reaches your desired consistency. Either way, mix everything together and taste for seasoning, adding a little more salt if necessary.

Chill and use as required, allowing a very heaped tablespoon per person for 100 g (3½ oz) pasta. Remember to toss with a little of the pasta cooking water, too.

Ciccioneddos, Tiny Tomatoes, Anchovies, Mascarpone and Basil

Serves 2

salt

200 g (7 oz) *ciccioneddo*, gnocchetti sardi or other similar pasta

4 tablespoons olive oil, plus extra to finish

1 garlic clove, halved

about 200 g (7 oz) (a large handful or a small punnet) small, sweet tomatoes (such as datterini or cherry)

6 or so anchovy fillets

2 tablespoons mascarpone

20 g (¾ oz) pecorino or Parmesan, grated

fresh basil, to finish

Ciccioneddo is Mauro's nickname for the people in his life he's fond of. It means, roughly, 'little fat one' in Sardinian. A small pasta shape often known as Sardinian *gnochetti*, being similar in their ridged, slightly maggot-like form to *malloreddus* (their larger, longer and better-known cousins), these chubby, stubby little nuggets are immensely satisfying to eat. If I were being romantic I'd say they looked like cowries, but perhaps they are really more like caterpillars.

The real joy of the *ciccioneddo* (apart from letting the word itself bounce like a small, fat caterpillar off the tongue) is that they are small enough for the finished dish to seem almost *soupy* (being easily swallowed whole without noticing) but big enough for it to still be toothily textural and feel like pasta not risotto. We are still firmly in fork territory here; no spoons in sight.

The bursting tomatoes are a revelatory way of creating an unctuous sauce without opening a tin and reducing its content down to maximise flavour. Little tomatoes, when ripe, have a concentrated sweetness, and thus once fried briefly in oil release intense, honey/vinegar juices, which emulsify with the olive oil to form an instant and rich sauce. Half a garlic clove or two is enough to give the sauce a background punch, and anchovies provide depth and savouriness. The intense tomato sauce is then cooled and made creamy by a swirl of mascarpone. I first read about the anchovy, mascarpone and tomato combination via a Nigella recipe (of course!). It has become a firm high-summer favourite because it is easy, quick, cheap and filling, and relies on only having a few fresh things to hand. The sauce can be made in the time it takes to cook the pasta.

Bring a large pan of salted water to the boil, then drop in your pasta.

Heat the olive oil in a sauté pan over a medium heat, add the garlic halves and cook until they sizzle and just begin to turn golden. Pierce your tomatoes with a knife and then throw them into the pan. Cook until they start to soften, pressing them down with your wooden spoon to help them collapse and release their juices (you can also add a splash of water here if it looks like things are catching). Once the tomatoes have burst, add the anchovies and melt them in, stirring. Now add the mascarpone and swirl.

Drain the pasta once *al dente*, reserving a little cooking water. Add the pasta to the pan with the sauce and a ladle or so of the reserved cooking water. Allow the whole lot to simmer for a minute or two. Stir in the grated cheese, sprinkle over some torn basil, add a splash or two more of water if necessary, drizzle with oil and serve.

Spaghettini with Burst Baby Tomatoes, Vernaccia, Bottarga and Parsley

Spaghettini del Sinis

Serves 2

salt

200 g (7 oz) spaghettini

about 6 tablespoons
extra virgin olive oil,
plus extra to finish

1 garlic clove, halved

200 g (7 oz) small tomatoes,
halved

1 small glass of Vernaccia,
dry sherry or vermouth

a nub of bottarga

a handful of parsley leaves,
roughly chopped

I can't pretend I don't feel funny writing the words burst and baby one after the other, because I do, but don't let my perverse sense of humour detract from what is a truly brilliant recipe.

Bottarga is made in the region around us, and I feel the need to talk about it again, because it is still underapppreciated and still one of Sardinia's greatest exports. Tomatoes and bottarga work together beautifully: both ingredients are packed with the sweet/savoury/saltiness often called umami, and the acidity of the tomatoes balances out the rich butteriness of the bottarga perfectly. Make sure you buy good ripe tomatoes.

Bring a large pan of well-salted water to the boil and add the spaghettini.

Pour the oil into a deep frying pan (skillet) and place over a medium-low heat. Add the garlic halves and allow to sizzle and just begin to colour, then throw in the tomato halves. Sizzle away, stirring occasionally, until the tomatoes collapse (add a splash of water if necessary). Now add the wine and simmer for a few minutes. (This whole process can be done before you cook the pasta, if you like. Alternatively, you can use the pasta cooking time – normally around 12 minutes – to make your sauce. If you have everything ready to go, this is perfectly feasible.)

Once *al dente*, drain the spaghettini, reserving a little cooking water. Toss the pasta into the pan with the tomatoes and add the bottarga and a splash or two of the cooking water. Keep stirring and tossing over a medium-low heat, adding more water if necessary, until the whole lot starts to look creamy (don't use a high heat as the bottarga will become grainy). When you have a nice creamy consistency, add a final drizzle of oil and the chopped parsley, stir briefly and serve.

Pasta Caprese

Serves 2 abundantly (you will eat lots)

200 g (7 oz) pasta (I use rigatoni or tortiglione)

450–500 g (1 lb–1 lb 2 oz) ripe tomatoes

a generous handful of basil leaves

1 garlic clove, halved

2 balls of mozzarella

extra virgin olive oil (plenty)

salt, to taste

The classic tricolour Caprese salad reimagined in a pasta dish, this is one of my staples of high summer. It involves making a messier version of the infamous Caprese salad, chopped tomatoes, some bruised garlic, plenty of oil, juicy mozzarella and basil, tossed through some good sturdy *al dente* pasta. It is so simple and so unbelievably good to eat: juicy, sweet, creamy, fragrant, dribbly happiness. Like all of the simplest recipes, the quality of the ingredients is tantamount: ripe tomatoes, a good oil. It's also important that the pasta is *al dente*, as eating in a salad it becomes extra important to have a bit of chew.

Cook the pasta in well-salted boiling water until *al dente*. Drain and allow to cool slightly, stirring occasionally to stop it sticking together.

Chop the tomatoes and add them with the torn basil and halved garlic to a large bowl big enough to hold everything. Tear in the mozzarella. Add a few good glugs of oil and a fair few pinches of salt. Toss everything well and taste for seasoning. Add more salt and more oil if necessary.

Serve.

COURGETTES

A much maligned vegetable, the courgette (*zucchini*). Perhaps because – at least to me – it was more commonly confused with a marrow. A marrow (a large courgette) was something my grandmother grew on the muck heap, picked, boiled, stuffed with mince and baked with béchamel to the point where you could really no longer tell it was anything other than a faintly green-striped vessel for other delicious, rich, fatty things. The marrow itself was considered cheap, easy and useful as a container, but was ridiculed as a vegetable in its own right. My grandmother grew them and they cropped so prolifically she made them into everything. She had a recipe for marrow and ginger jam, which was highly prized, and my uncle even made them into wine as part of his adolescent alcoholic experiments. The sight of a large marrow on the kitchen worktop was treated with scorn and glee in equal measure; stuffed marrow we loved, but the marrow itself was always viewed as a sorry thing, more bitter water than firm, tasty flesh.

Glamorous it was not, but loved by those with old souls such as my grandmother and my father, both of whom grew up with the classic post-war mentality of not wasting anything, and making meals out of practically nothing. The marrow is the bedfellow of thrift; a giant vegetable that can feed a hungry family for days, which – when growing – practically thrives on neglect.

But now I have the left the land of marrows behind me, and here in Italy we have the much more glamorous *zucchini*, which is really just a small marrow with better PR. Everybody knows when it comes to fruit and vegetables, the smaller the better. Bigger fruit, bigger vegetables as a general rule simply means less flavour. The inherent flavour (most often sweetness/nuttiness/earthiness) is distributed over a greater surface area and diluted by more water, which is why chefs fetishise tiny/baby vegetables – not just because they look adorable but because (in theory) their flavour should be concentrated. However, as every good gardener/grower knows, tiny vegetables means less yield. Harvesting things when they are small means

they don't go as far where meals are concerned, so – like everything in life – one must find a compromise.

My grandmother, once she was too old to either have a proper vegetable garden or care much about anything other than behaving outrageously and relishing the small pleasures left to her, would plant a handful of carrots and potatoes in pots outside the back door, dig them up voraciously when they were still minute, boil them and butter them generously, and we would feast like kings for one glorious night alone, on tiny, perfect vegetables that tasted of parodies of themselves.

But back to the courgettes. Courgettes are at their best when they are small. The smaller varieties are so sweet and nutty when fresh they are delicious eaten raw; made into salads or fried/grilled briefly to highlight their nuttiness. Medium-sized courgettes can be sautéed, fried or made into pasta dishes/sauces, and larger ones hollowed and stuffed with flavoursome fillings. They are infinitely adaptable and utterly delicious whichever way you cook them. I think – if pressed – I would say they are one of my favourite vegetables, as their versatility means they occupy a large place in my heart. They are rarely bitter, as they once were, and add beautiful colours and shapes to the plate, too.

The *zucchini* in Italy is well loved, respected and understood, but it has been slow to win over the UK – perhaps due to memories of marrows. Nevertheless, the courgette deserves to be appreciated for what it is, and the many gifts it gives the cook. What is so often dismissed as 'wateriness' is really a great gift; when cooked well the courgette collapses into a delicious sweet and vegetal juice, which when eaten alongside the Chicken with Two Lemons on p.219 provides a sort of wonderful silky, sweet sauce, meaning there is no need to faff around making gravy or jus or anything so ludicrous when you have juicy meat and juicy vegetables, and the essential trickle of punchy olive oil.

After making the following recipes, I very much hope you will never look down on a courgette again.

Ricotta, Lemon and Herb-stuffed Zucchini Flowers

Serves 4

250 g (9 oz) ricotta

25 g (1 oz) Parmesan/pecorino, grated

zest of 1 small lemon

a good few leaves of mint, parsley and basil, roughly chopped

salt and black pepper, to taste

8 baby courgettes (zucchini) with flowers attached

sunflower oil, for deep-frying

lemon wedges, to serve

For the batter

110 ml (3¾ floz/scant ½ cup) cold fizzy water (of your preference)

80 g (3 oz/¾ cup) '00' flour

a pinch of salt

1–2 ice cubes

My first foray into gardening was during Covid, when I decided to plant a small *orto* (plot) of my own. Knowing my own limits, I stuck firmly to the two things it is (supposedly) nearly impossible not to succeed with: radishes and courgettes (zucchini). The courgettes flowered furiously, but I quickly realised that none of the flowers went on to become courgettes. They were all male plants, which produce only the golden trumpets, while the females produce the fruit (or vegetable). As both male and female plants produce flowers ideal for stuffing, you can use either for this recipe, but when I can get baby courgettes with both flower and small tender fruit, I like to fry these, as they make more of a meal.

You can use supermarket tub ricotta for this if you like, or the real stuff. They can be made a day or two in advance and kept in the refrigerator before frying.

Drain the ricotta well (if sitting in liquid) and mix in the grated cheese, lemon zest, chopped herbs and salt and pepper. Taste for seasoning and add more lemon/cheese/salt as fitting. It should be nicely seasoned – cheesy, creamy and herby.

Carefully prise open the delicate courgette flowers and remove the stubby yellow stamen within (they should snap off quite neatly). Using a teaspoon, fill each bud well with the filling and then seal the petals around it, twisting them at the top. Place in the refrigerator to firm up until ready to serve (they can sit for a day or two here quite happily).

Prepare a simple batter by mixing the fizzy water gently into the flour and salt, whisking gently to create a smooth mixture. Add the last few drops of water slowly and mix very gently to help maintain some fizz. Add the ice cubes (these are not essential but help the finished fried things stay extra crispy).

Heat enough oil for deep-frying to around 180°C (350°F), or until a wooden spoon creates bubbles when placed into it.

Dip the flowers briefly into the batter and then drop them gently into the oil. Fry until golden, then remove with a slotted spoon to drain on some paper towels.

Serve with a wedge of lemon, a side salad, some bread and a beer.

Buttered Courgette Spaghetti

Spaghetti alla Stanley (or A Study in Simplicity)

Serves 2

2 courgettes (zucchini), trimmed

olive oil, for frying

sea salt, for sprinkling

spaghetti for two

a knob of butter

Parmesan, for grating

I can't remember where I read this allegory, but it stuck with me, stubborn as a sesame seed trapped in your teeth.

A lady walks into a hat shop. She looks at a number of elaborate hats; hats with tassles and ribbons and flowers and stuffed birds. She browses the selection and then her eye catches a small, simple, perfectly formed trilby tucked away in the corner. She looks at the price tag. It is the most expensive hat in the shop. She summons the shop owner.

'Why is this hat so expensive?' she asks.

'Well,' he replies with a wry smile, 'Madam is paying for the restraint.'

I love this story and try to apply it often to my cooking, my writing, almost everything I do. It is so often tempting to add more, to think that embellishment automatically adds aesthetic value. Often it is the removal of elaboration, the stripping down and taking away that is more poignant and effective. In terms of Italian cookery specifically, it is almost always simplicity and minimalism that paves the way to success.

I found out about this way of making the silkiest sauce for spaghetti via a friend who is a devout watcher of Stanley Tucci's *Searching for Italy*. She and her friends recreated the zucchini sauce featured on his Amalfi episode and raved about it to such an extent that I knew I had to recreate it. The dish is mind-blowingly simple. A perfect example of the cunning and minimalism that is the core of Italian cookery.

The slow frying of the zucchini in the pan (in theory the zucchini are deep-fried, but I don't find it necessary here) releases their elusive sweet and savoury juices and creates the most divine silky sauce for coating strands of spaghetti. There is no onion added, no garlic, no herbs. No lemon. Just a little bit of butter and some cheese. The zucchini is left overnight, which is fundamental, as this allows the flavours to develop.

Such simplicity requires great courage; it is all too easy to fall back on the help of highly flavoured ingredients. When I make it, it takes all my will power not to add a pinch of chilli, a sliver of garlic. But Madam is paying for the restraint. The result is silky, sensational, Stanley-worthy spaghetti. There is no need to give precise quantities for this recipe because it is too simple to even weigh up.

The night before you want to eat, slice the courgettes into thin rounds/ crescents. If large, deseed first and use only the flesh.

Heat the oil in a large, deep frying pan (skillet) over a low heat and scatter over the courgette slices. Fry them slowly, tossing occasionally, making sure not to let anything become too dark. This will take about 20–30 minutes. They should be completely wilted, translucent with oil, and a good golden colour all over. Remove to a plate, sprinkle with salt and set aside (in the refrigerator or somewhere cool).

The next day, when you are ready to eat, bring a large pan of salted water to the boil.

In a frying pan, heat another good glug of olive oil (at this point you can either blend the courgettes in a blender or with a stick blender if you want this to be a smoother affair, or just leave to break down a little in the pan). Warm the courgettes in the oil while you drop your spaghetti into the boiling water to cook until al dente.

Add a knob of butter to the courgettes and remove from the heat. Scoop the cooked spaghetti straight into the frying pan, along with some of the cooking water. Stir and toss and stir and toss until everything is smooth and creamy and all the strands are silky and glistening. Add a brief blizzard of freshly grated Parmesan and serve.

Eat. And behold the Word of Stanley made flesh.

Courgette, Ginger and Lemon Confit/Jam

Makes 2 small jam jars

450 g (1 lb) prepared marrow
or large courgettes (zucchini)
(weight after deseeding)

1 lemon

250 ml (8½ fl oz/1 cup) water

250 g (9 oz/generous 1 cup)
sugar

20 g (¾ oz) fresh root ginger,
peeled and finely grated

It felt wrong to call this a jam, exactly, because it sort of exists in a golden-yellow class of its own. If a jam carries implications of uniform texture and firm-ish set, then it would be highly misleading to label this as such. More like a confit perhaps, this golden liquid containing suspended amber cubes of candied marrow/courgette (zucchini) never sets beyond syrupy, but that is part of its charm.

Let me count the ways in which I love this confit. One of them, of course, being the memory of my grandmother and her famous marrows, another being that it tastes wonderfully of lemon and I adore lemons; another that it is the most beautiful thing to look at, has an otherworldly flavour and uses up all those burgeoning courgettes that balloon and bulge overnight absorbing who knows what water from where, considering the ground is so hot and dry you could grill a steak on it.

It may sound odd, but in terms of flavour you almost don't know the courgette is there at all; a classic case of something being essential and simultaneously almost indiscernible. You'd know if it wasn't there, the end result being a vague gingery lemon syrup, but it is very hard to put your finger on what it adds apart from body and texture. There is something citrussy about courgettes when they are raw, a whiff of lemon and young almond, and this jam celebrates that quality. As I say, the courgette has many faces, and all of them are interesting.

This is very special served in a tender Victoria sponge (p.144) with some very softly whipped cream, or with thick yoghurt for a summery breakfast, or on warm scones with a little salty butter. My grandmother used to serve it on pancakes, too.

Sterilise your jars by boiling them in boiling water for a few minutes. Place a couple of saucers in the refrigerator to test the setting point later.

Cut the prepared marrow/courgette flesh (with the skin) into small pieces, about the size of a sugar cube. Zest the lemon and set aside. Squeeze the juice, then place the spent lemon halves in a muslin (cheesecloth) bag tied with string.

Cook the marrow/courgette in the measured water, covered, over a low heat until translucent (this will take about 10 minutes). Add the sugar, the grated lemon zest and juice, the grated ginger and the muslin bag with the lemon halves. Cook at a low simmer for around 50 minutes–1 hour, then test for a set (dribble a little of the liquid onto one of the cold saucers, wait for 10 seconds, then push your finger through it – if wrinkles form you have reached setting point). Keep cooking if there are no wrinkles and repeat the setting test as necessary.

Pot and store for at least a few days (in a cool, dark place) before opening.

Courgette Ginger Cake with Lemon, Yoghurt and Mascarpone Icing

Serves 8–10

200 g (7 oz) courgettes
(zucchini)

100 g (3½ oz) butter, at room
temperature, plus extra
for greasing

90 ml (3 fl oz/⅓ cup) olive oil

230 g (8 oz/1 cup) sugar

3 eggs

1 scant teaspoon salt

2 teaspoons ground ginger
or 1 tablespoon freshly grated
root ginger

250 g (9 oz/2¼ cups) '00' flour

1 tablespoon baking powder

zest and juice of 1 large lemon
or 2 small, plus extra zest
to decorate

3 tablespoons thick (Greek)
yoghurt

blackberries, to decorate
(optional)

edible flowers and leaves, to
decorate (optional)

For the icing (frosting)

250 g (9 oz/1 generous cup)
mascarpone

100 g (3½ oz/generous ¾ cup)
icing (confectioners') sugar

zest of 1 lemon,
plus 4 teaspoons juice

100 g (3½ oz/generous ⅓ cup)
thick (Greek) yoghurt

This cake has the most sublime texture and tastes like the very essence of summer. Lemony light, damply sweet from the courgettes (zucchini) and with a wonderful cloud-whip of tangy icing (frosting) it is the perfect cake for a long summer afternoon.

It is also very good at breakfast without the icing (plain with a dollop of yoghurt, or with a simple lemon glaze, p.128, would be nice), very good at teatime or for occasions. A highly adaptable, fresh and fruity cake, moist and zesty, just-flecked with pale green, and a great way of using up endless courgettes. If you have fresh ginger readily available you can use that, too. It creates an even more vibrant flavour.

Any extra icing can be used as a little mousse alongside some summer berries.

Top and tail the courgettes, then finely grate them into a colander over the sink, squeezing out excess juice with your hands.

Preheat the oven to 180°C (350°F/gas 4). Grease and line a 23 cm (9 in) springform cake tin (pan) with baking paper.

Beat the butter and oil together with the sugar until pale, smooth and fluffy. Add the eggs, one at a time, beating well after each addition until they are fully incorporated. Add the salt, ginger, flour, baking powder, courgettes, lemon zest and juice, and yoghurt, and stir to combine.

Spoon the batter into the prepared tin and bake for 40-50 minutes until risen and golden, and an inserted skewer comes out clean (turn the oven down halfway through if the cake looks as though it's taking on too much colour).

Remove from the oven and allow to cool for 10 minutes before turning out of the tin and leaving to cool completely on a wire rack.

For the icing, beat the mascarpone with the icing sugar, then add the lemon zest and juice and yoghurt, and beat again until smooth. Spread evenly over the top of the cake. Decorate with lemon zest, blackberries and edible flowers, if you like.

A True Sardinian Bicicletta

Serves 1

1 bottle of Sanbitter (you can use a Campari Soda if you can't find it)

60 ml or so (2 fl oz/¼ cup) Vernaccia (or preferred white wine)

a few large ice cubes

a fat slice of fresh Sardinian lemon

The *Bicicletta* is a lesser-known spritz with a secret Sardinian following, a genius name and a few essential twists to differentiate it from the standard bitter-sweet and jewel-like aperitivos you might already know and love.

The Bicicletta is technically a spritz, but instead of using Aperol, a bright-orange 'bitter' made from gentian, rhubarb and cinchona among other things, the Sardinian version uses Sanbitter, a premixed bitter (which is non-alcoholic) and then a healthy glug of local young Vernaccia, to fortify things.

The fundamental elements of the finest spritz are there; it is strong, thirst-quenching, bitter, sweet. It is deep and fierce and fiery-red. It is also refreshing, thanks to the Vernaccia (or white wine) and soda, meaning it can be sipped with a wry smile rather than hurriedly knocked back through gritted teeth. It is sort of somewhere between a negroni and a Campari Soda, with some of the smooth and sophisticated force of the former, and some of the refreshing bitter-sweetness of the latter. The Vernaccia's eccentric almondy undertones add an inimitable Sardinian twist. Mauro insists it must have a slice of lemon, too, as a garnish, rather than the more common orange.

Its name, however, is probably my favourite thing about this eccentric spritz. Named after the folkloristic old men who frequent the oldest bars all over Italy, this — as the legend goes — was their beverage of choice as they whiled away the sleepy golden afternoons, before weaving their way home, singing gentle snatches of songs to themselves between the occasional hiccup. Anyone who has spent any time in any part of Italy will know such bars well, just as they will know such old men on bicycles. Perhaps a flat cap, a withered cigarette perennially hanging from one corner of their mouths, and a wooden vegetable crate mounted over the back wheel, held in place with a bungee rope. Perhaps a plant bulb or two or some twine in the crate. The type of bar where — as Mauro fondly remembers — in the good old days you couldn't see your hand in front of you for the dense fog of cigarette smoke. In our village bar, one local man — Guido — used to bring his beloved pet sheep in for a Bicicletta with him.

Mix in the glass, sip, savour. With or without pet sheep.

AUTUMN

Autunno

Rains and Saints

Just as the heat becomes unbearable, the rains come and break the spell of summer. A short season, *l'autunno*, it functions as a sort of damp pause between the lengthy hedonism of summer, which has just begun to wane, and the hibernation and hardship of winter.

Before the rain comes the grape harvest, the *Vendemmia*, which usually happens in mid- to late-September, depending on how ripe the fruit is. Mauro picks samples and tests their sugar levels. We cannot harvest until they reach a certain percentage of sugar, as this is what will allow the wine to age as it should, and have the characteristic flavour that makes it so unique.

The grapes are sticky with juice, just blotted brown in patches by the heat of the sun. 'These are the best ones to eat,' says Lorenzo, plucking a brown-smudged cluster: 'like caramels.' The sweetness is intense, more sweet even than caramel: a sweetness only sun can produce. Zio Mario, Mauro's uncle, is in the vines too. He pretends he is just passing by chance but we know he drives his Punto around all day, hoping to bump into us, so he can hop out to help and pretend he wasn't dying to do so. As we pick he tells stories from a childhood spent in *campagna*, over 70 years ago, stories of foxes and rabbits and hunting and harvests and weaving baskets out of willow. He produces his trademark contribution to the *Vendemmia*, a bottle of *gassosa* (suspiciously clear lemonade), which we all drink gratefully, parched from picking.

If the Maestrale blows it is pleasant work and we eat as we go, getting stickier by the second. As the sun hits the grapes they glow as if with internal light, like pale, green-golden beads. Vernaccia grapes are beautiful, rounder and more golden than other white varieties like Muscat. They are noticeably sweeter too; honeyed.

We work our way along the rows, Zio keeping up a constant background discourse, then load the crates onto the trailer and head home for lunch. Some days, if we are organised, we bring a picnic with us, or grill steaks out in the vineyard. This is the traditional *Vendemmia* lunch, eaten outside in the shade of the olives. Two weeks of picking, and then it is done.

Then comes the rain; November awash with day after day of it. The pale grey ink of the sky bleeds into the sea, and we fear the tortoises will wash away. The last roses droop heavy with fat droplets. The golden landscape becomes green again, and we complain — between secret sighs of relief, for this rain is needed. There are quinces; golden, furred and perfumed, brown and puckered at both ends. There are pumpkins and persimmons too, and best of all there are chestnuts for roasting and eating on the street.

It is the time of the year that I start to hear that familiar phrase, *domani e festa*, again, as Saints days accumulate, and the Christian calendar kicks into gear once more after its carefree heathen summer by the sea. The crowning festival of autumn is All Saints, or *Ognissanti*, when traditional dishes such as the *Lorighittas* on p.184 are prepared and eaten. Spiced cookies are made with the grape syrup (*sapa*) from the harvest, and the smell of frying is in the air, as we once again take comfort in food to *coccolare* (cuddle, pamper or coddle/cosset) the soul, and keep the cold at bay.

FETTERIA ROMA
olce Risveglio

Roast Squash, Dark Chocolate, Olive Oil and Clementine Cake

Makes 1 large loaf cake

1 medium squash (use a dry creamy squash, such as an onion squash; if you have to use a watery one, drain it after roasting)

For the cake

melted butter or baking spray, for greasing

230 g (8 oz/1¾ cups) plain (all-purpose) or '00' flour

3 teaspoons baking powder

1 teaspoon ground cinnamon

2 teaspoons ground nutmeg

1 teaspoon salt

230 ml (8 fl oz/scant 1 cup) olive oil

230 g (8 oz/1 cup) sugar

grated zest of 2 clementines or 1 orange

3 eggs

150 g (5 oz) dark chocolate, roughly chopped

For the glaze

1½ tablespoons orange juice

1½ tablespoons olive oil

150 g (5 oz/1¼ cups) icing (confectioners') sugar

To decorate (optional)

pomegranate seeds

pumpkin seeds

orange zest

dark chocolate shards or cacao nibs

This is an extraordinary cake. I can't claim to have invented it, as much as I would like to, but of course I have changed it (almost) beyond recognition. It has a vivid orange crumb – so soft, impossibly soft, so moist and spicy and deep and earthy and fresh and zingy and autumnal and grounded by the rich dark rumble of chocolate and an echo of grassy green olive oil.

It could be a breakfast cake, a tea cake, a Christmas cake, a November cake, a Sunday cake, a pudding cake. An everything cake. Even the cat likes it.

Preheat the oven to 220°C (425°F/gas 7).

Cut the squash down the middle, scoop out the seeds and place it cut-side down on a non-stick baking tray (pan) (you can line with baking paper if you prefer – there may be some sticky caramelised squash bits to scrub). Roast for 30–45 minutes until completely soft (it will magically steam itself).

Scrape the squash flesh away from the skin and purée in a blender until smooth. Measure out 230 g (8 oz) of the purée (use the rest as you see fit) and let it cool.

Reduce the oven to 170°C (325°F/gas 3) and thoroughly grease a large 900-g (2-lb) loaf tin (pan) with melted butter and a pastry brush (make sure you get every crevice, you can use a baking spray, if you prefer).

Sift the flour, baking powder, ground spices and salt together in a bowl. In a separate bowl, whisk together the oil, sugar, zest and eggs with the cooled squash purée. Make a well in the centre of the flour mixture and whisk in the wet ingredients until you have a smooth batter. Stir in the chocolate pieces.

Pour the batter into the prepared loaf tin and bake for up to 1½ hours, or until an inserted skewer comes out clean. Allow to cool before turning out.

For the glaze, mix the orange juice and olive oil with the icing sugar until you have a glaze the consistency of honey. Pour over the cooled cake.

Decorate with pomegranate or pumpkin seeds or orange zest, or with extra chocolate shards/cacao nibs.

Pumpkin Gnocchi Fried in Sage Butter

Serves 4 as a starter or 2 as a main

1 kg (2 lb 4 oz) delica pumpkin
salt
olive oil
1 egg yolk
40 g (1½ oz) grated Parmesan, plus extra to serve
a scrape or two of lemon zest (optional but I like it – it offsets the sweetness of the pumpkin)
a few scrapings of nutmeg
100–150 g (3½–5oz/ generous ¾–1¼ cups) plain (all-purpose) flour, plus extra for dusting

To serve

80 g (3 oz) butter
a few sage leaves
a squeeze of lemon juice
grated roasted hazelnuts/ walnuts (optional)

Gnocchi are underappreciated, delicious and extremely useful things to have up a cook's sleeve. People are put off from making them, perhaps, by the inevitable fear of collapse, the terrifying moment as you plop them into a pan of rolling boiling water, peering timorously over the lip, watching it cloud and swirl, and then breathing a sigh of relief as the pluckly little dumpling rises to the surface. Sometimes this bobbing doesn't happen at all, and the *gnocco* simply dissolves into a sad, watery cloud, never bobbing to the surface. This recipe doesn't do that.

Pure pumpkin is best, both for flavour and colour (I do not add potato). The variety of pumpkin is very important, too – it can't be watery. The egg yolk helps to bind and adds richness, and keeping flour to a minimal amount prevents things getting too stodgy. A good *gnocco* should be toothsome and chewy but not gummy, and still have a bouncing lightness to it. The secret lies in light handling, not too much flour and eating them fresh. Not made to keep, they need to be made and cooked *alla minute*.

People who find pumpkin too sweet will be mollified with the inescapably savoury sage butter and extra cheese on serving.

Preheat the oven to 180°C (350°F/gas 4).

Cut the pumpkin into six wedges and discard the seeds (no need to peel). Place on a lined baking tray (pan) and sprinkle with salt. Drizzle over a little olive oil, cover with foil and roast for around 30 minutes until just beginning to soften. Remove the foil and cook for another 15 minutes or so until completely tender and just beginning to colour at the edges.

Remove from the oven. Once cool enough to handle, scrape the flesh into a bowl. Mash it well with a fork until smooth and leave to cool.

Once cool, add the egg yolk and the cheese, then the lemon zest and nutmeg and taste for seasoning, adjusting accordingly. They need to be generously seasoned. Add the flour, starting with 100 g (3½ oz/generous ¾ cup) initially and only adding more if you think it is needed. Mix gently until you have a dough that is soft but not too sticky to handle (the consistency of mashed potato). Flour your work surface and shape the dough into fat sausages, about 2.5 cm (1 in) wide. Cut each sausage into 2.5 cm (1 in) nuggets and set aside on a floured tray/work surface/board.

Bring a large pan of salted water to the boil and plop the *gnocchi* in. After a couple of minutes, when they bob to the surface, remove with a slotted spoon and set aside, tossing occasionally to ensure they don't stick together (at this point you can toss them with olive oil and store them in the refrigerator for later, if you like).

Warm the butter in a sauté pan and add the sage leaves, then add the gnocchi and sauté until just beginning to brown. Season with salt and a squeeze of lemon juice, then serve with some grated Parmesan or grated roasted hazelnuts/walnuts.

Autumn

Lorighittas with Chicken Ragù

Serves 4

In Morgongiori, a small town south of Oristano at the base of Monte Arci, its surrounds dotted with *corbezzolo* trees, a very rare, special and unique pasta is made. *Lorighittas* are tiny little braided loops, made by twisting two individual strands of simple *semola*-and-water dough together, then joining them in a ring. Their name derives from the word *loriga*, which means 'ring' or 'earring' in Sardinian.

They are traditionally made and eaten around the period of All Saints, or *Ognissanti*, which falls on 1 November, when the women of the village would gather to *impastare* (make and knead dough), and with busy, deft fingers form thousands of the little filigreed loops.

Made only in this small town, and now by a mere handful of women, the *lorighitta* is one of the most striking pasta shapes in the world, and one of the hardest to make. Made entirely by hand (there is no machine that can imitate the intricate twists), they are incredibly time-consuming, but indisputably beautiful. Gilda is one of the few women still making *lorighittas* regularly in Morgongiori. She used to run an *agriturismo* called Sa Lorighitta, where she made her own bread, cheese and sausages, grew all of her own vegetables and still found the time to make *lorighittas* nearly every day. She tells me through a proud grin that in all her 20 years running the *agriturismo* she never once served a customer a plate of pasta that wasn't made by her own hands (not just the sauce but the pasta itself). She made *lorighittas* by the hundreds, as she still does now, though mostly for friends and family.

I watch her work. She begins by making a simple, relatively firm dough out of locally milled fine *semola*, water and a pinch of salt. Decanting the *semola* into a traditional terracotta pasta bowl known as a *xivedda,* she sprinkles the salt, making the sign of the cross in the sandy golden mound before adding the water. She says before she begins to *impastare*, whether she is making bread or pasta, she always makes the sign of the cross. After adding the water she brings the dough together, then removes it from the bowl and places it on the wooden table before beginning to knead. She kneads vigorously for at least 20 minutes or so, chatting busily, her arms working with a strength wholly unexpected considering her diminutive frame. As she recounts stories of her childhood, interspersed with the occasional traditional folksong or chanted poetry, her contagious smile fixed throughout, she remembers her mother killing a pig around this time every winter (pig killing was women's work) and the lard (*strutto*) that was made was used to fry fresh doughnuts at home. She rolls her eyes into the back of her head with pleasure as she remembers the smell and flavour of those doughnuts, and the flavour of the pig meat, which she often used to make a sauce for her *lorighittas*. The most traditional sauce for *lorighittas* is a simple chicken and tomato ragù, made with a little onion, a home-reared chicken and tinned tomatoes. These are usually the only

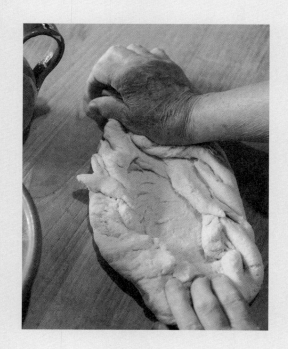

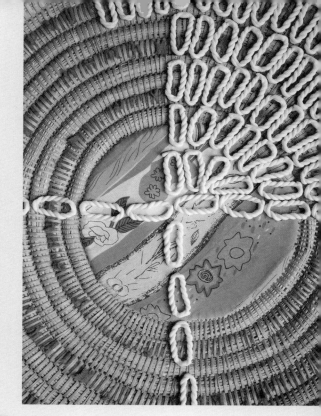

For the dough

400 g (14 oz/generous 3 cups) *semola* (semolina)

a pinch of salt

190–200 ml (6½–7 fl oz/ generous ¾–scant 1 cup) water

For the ragù

2 tablespoons olive oil

½ white onion, diced

around ½ chicken with bones (about 800 g/1 lb 12 oz) (nice and free-range, organic and lively), chopped into apricot-sized pieces on the bone

800 g (1 lb 12 oz) tinned tomatoes

salt

ingredients, but the length of cooking and the inherent flavour of a good chicken are enough to make a sauce that is deeply flavoursome, complex and comforting. The *lorighittas* provide the perfect foil, sturdy and chewy and catching the sauce in their prolific cracks and weaves, they remain wonderfully and deliciously *al dente* in the centre. There are really only five ingredients in this dish: chicken, olive oil, onion, tomatoes and pasta. The most important ingredient, as is so often the case in Sardinia, is *time. Al fuogo lentu*, as they say in Sardinian, 'over a slow flame'. This could be the title of our communal autobiography.

After Gilda has finished working her dough she rests it, then begins to shape it; first rolled out to thin, spaghetti-like lengths, then a small length is pinched off, wrapped twice around two fingers, then tiny twists of the fingertips twirl each little double-stranded band into a braid. In mere seconds the top is sealed and a perfect *lorighitta* laid on the base of a traditional basket. They are best dried *Al sole*, says Gilda, *Like we used to do. We'd put them out on the roof to dry under the sun.* These days 'health and safety' won't allow it, but she can taste the difference between pasta dried in the sun and pasta dried in an oven.

You can have a go at making *lorighittas* using the following dough recipe, or see if you can get hold of a packet. Alternatively, this sauce can be paired with your favourite pasta shape.

To make the pasta dough, mix the *semola* and salt, then pour in the water. Mix with your hands to form a rough dough, then remove from the bowl and begin to knead on the work surface. Knead to form a smooth dough – this will take around 10–20 minutes. Once smooth and uniform, set aside, covered or wrapped in a bag, to rest for about 30 minutes.

Once ready to shape, break off lengths of the dough and roll them out using the palms of your hands to form long, spaghetti-like strands. Break off a 7.5 cm (3 in) length, wrap twice around your fore- and middle fingers and seal the ends. Using your other forefinger and thumb, twist to form little braids. Lay out to dry.

To make the ragù, heat the oil in a heavy-based saucepan over a low heat. Add the onion and begin to sauté, stirring occasionally, until translucent. Add the chicken pieces, increase the heat to medium and continue to sauté, allowing the chicken to get some golden colour (especially on the skin). After about 10 minutes or so, add the tomatoes. Turn the heat down to the lowest simmer, cover and cook for about 1 hour until the sauce is reduced and flavoursome and the chicken is soft and giving and melting off the bone.

Just before you are ready to serve, cook your *lorighittas* in plenty of boiling salted water until *al dente*, then drain and add to the sauce, and cook through for the final few minutes.

Rigatoni with Parsley, Pecorino, Ricotta and Walnut Pesto

Serves 2

100 g (3½ oz/1 cup) walnuts

1 small garlic clove, peeled

40 g (1½ oz) pecorino, grated, plus extra to serve

40 g (1½ oz) Parmesan, grated, plus extra to serve

1 small bunch of flat-leaf parsley, leaves finely chopped

120 g (4 oz) ricotta

200 g (7 oz) smooth rigatoni or pasta of choice

salt

extra virgin olive oil, to serve

Walnuts are underappreciated; I love their tannic tang and milky, freshly cut endive bitterness, and the undertones of wood and fires. They work so well in a pesto, making it undeniably wintry and none the worse for that. The ricotta melts to form a cream that binds the whole dish together even if your walnuts are on the chunky side, as mine were, having bashed them all by hand. Parsley, too, is a herb that's at home in all seasons, unlike the undeniably high-summer basil. You could use a little cream, if you liked, instead of the ricotta. This is also a pesto that works very well with pasta made with chestnut flour, as the sweet nuttiness of the flour balances the slight bitterness of the walnuts perfectly.

Note: Pesto is not just for pasta. It also works very well on grilled vegetables, this one in particular would be very good on roasted squash or pumpkin, or stirred into a soup.

Bash/pound or blitz the walnuts (if you like you can toast them first for a more intense flavour – 10 minutes in a 170°C (325°F/gas 3) oven; I keep them untoasted) with the garlic and a good pinch of salt. Stir in the pecorino and Parmesan, and then the finely chopped parsley (or blitz this in if using a blender). Let the ricotta down with a tablespoon or two of hot water and whisk it well until smooth. Stir or blitz it through the mixture.

Bring a pan of well-salted water to the boil and drop in the pasta of your choice (I use smooth rigatoni, sometimes called *maccherone* here, as I like smooth pasta with pesto – don't ask me why). Cook until *al dente*, then drain, reserving a little of the cooking water.

Stir your pesto into the pasta, adding a ladle of the cooking water and tossing and stirring well until you have a creamy sauce. Serve, with extra cheese and a drizzle of extra virgin olive oil.

Pina's Walnut and Honey Cake

Torta di Noci di Pina

Makes one 23 cm (9 in) cake

oil or butter, for greasing

300 g (10½ oz/3 cups) walnuts

3 eggs

300 g (10½ oz/1⅓ cups) sugar

300 g (10½ oz/2½ cups) plain (all-purpose) flour

2 teaspoons baking powder

a pinch of salt

100 g (3½ oz) butter

2 tablespoons honey

grated zest of 1 large orange

icing (confectioners') sugar, for dusting

Variations:

Add a spoonful of dark cocoa powder or some finely chopped very dark chocolate for a twist. Or trying using different honeys and see if they make a difference. I use my favourite *macchia Mediterranea* honey, which has a taste of smoked barley and works wonderfully in this.

A cake of humble appearance but great depth and goodness. Walnuts are the most underrated of nuts; their bittersweet oil making them a welcome and addictive addition to any sweet or savoury dish. Used in cakes, they contribute a rich, smoky depth of flavour and a wonderfully moist texture, their slight bitterness offset by the sugar. This cake, where they are combined with their natural bedfellow, honey, is simple, moist and delightful; chewy and a little dense in texture like a sort of honey-walnut brownie; the perfect thing to serve in dainty squares with black coffee at the end of a meal or to eat with a breakfast cappuccino.

Not only are the nuts beautiful, but the walnut trees too. My whole life I dreamt of a walnut tree and now we have one in *campagna*, with its long, slender and waxy leaves, and the clusters of smooth green nuts in their shells. We pick them in late summer, just as the green skin starts to brown and leave them in the sun to dry, before breaking them out completely and drying them again in the early autumn sun. The green husks can be boiled to make a dark sepia ink, which is said to have been used by Leonardo Da Vinci, and the shells themselves, when split into neat halves, provided endless fun for us as children, as we used them as miniature boats for tiny toy mice or Lego men.

It is important to remember that nuts have a shelf-life, and like many things their flavour changes over time. Fresh walnuts from a tree are milky and sweet and sappy, like a freshly picked dandelion or green fig, whereas those that have been sitting in bags for months will taste more dusty and of cupboards. Also the orange is important – try to get a good unwaxed one, which will have more fragrant zest. This is an equal quantities recipe, so feel free to scale up or scale down as you prefer (2 eggs, 200 g of everything else, etc.).

Preheat the oven to 180°C (350°F/gas 4). Grease and line a 23 cm (9 in) cake tin (pan) with baking paper.

Crush the nuts in a bag by banging them well with a rolling pin, leaving some pieces slightly bigger than others (Pina says this makes all the difference).

Whisk the eggs with the sugar until they are thick and moussey, then gently fold in the flour, baking powder, salt and crushed nuts.

Gently melt the butter, then stir through the honey and add the mixture to the batter along with the orange zest. Stir to combine.

Scoop the batter into your prepared tin and bake for 20–30 minutes. It will be brown on the top and slightly uneven due to the nuts, but that's good. Leave to cool in the tin for a few minutes, then turn out onto a wire rack to cool completely.

Slice into small squares/slices and dust with icing sugar before serving.

Sausage Lasagne with Ricotta, Pecorino and Fennel

Serves 6–8

For the ragù

3 tablespoons extra virgin olive oil

1 white onion, diced

2 garlic cloves, sliced

3–4 sage leaves

2 bay leaves

a sprig of rosemary

a sprig or two of wild fennel or a good pinch of fennel seeds

a good pinch of dried chilli

500 g (1 lb 2 oz) good-quality Italian sausagemeat, removed from its casing

2 glasses of white wine

800 g (1 lb 12 oz) tinned tomatoes

salt and pepper

To finish

12 dried egg lasagne sheets

350 g (12 oz) ricotta

4–5 tablespoons whole milk

60 g (2 oz) pecorino, grated

wild fennel fronds, to garnish (optional)

a drizzle of olive oil

A rich sausage ragu rivals a classic one, the fatty and flavoursome meat providing profound, garlic-scented depth. Here it is spiked with fennel, a good friend of the pig, and layered in a lasagne, with a sort of cheat's béchamel topping, which is quick, easy and possibly more delicious. The ragù needs a little time to cook down to goodness, but otherwise this is a very speedy assembly.

Begin by making the ragù. Heat the olive oil in a sauté pan over a medium heat, then sauté the onion and garlic until soft and translucent. Add the herbs, fennel and chilli, and sauté for a few minutes more, then add the sausagemeat. Sauté for a few minutes until the sausage begins to become golden, then add the wine and allow to simmer for a few minutes. Now add the tomatoes, rinsing each tin out with water and adding it to the pot. Leave to simmer and bubble away for about 30 minutes, a little longer if you have time. Taste and season accordingly. It should have reduced to a nice saucy consistency and taste flavoursome.

Preheat the oven to 190°C (375°F/gas 5).

Place a third of the ragù in a large gratin dish, then lay over a third of the lasagne sheets to cover. Add another layer of ragù, then another layer of pasta, then a final layer of ragù and a final layer of pasta.

Whisk the ricotta with the milk until creamy, and season with salt and pepper. Spread it over the top layer of pasta and sprinkle over the grated cheese. Lay over the fennel fronds (if using) and drizzle with some olive oil.

Place in the oven and cook for 40-45 minutes until golden and bubbling.

LA VERNACCIA DI ORISTANO, DOC

I could write a whole book on Vernaccia, just with the information I have gleaned from Mauro. I wish *he* would write a book about it, but he won't because he always – like me – has 'too many things in the *padella*' (frying pan).

He's a busy man, who holds down another job as well as spending all his spare waking hours making wine, in the way that his father and grandfather taught him. For him it is a passion, a need, an addiction almost. His veins flow with a mix of blood and Vernaccia.

'*Quando sono in Campagna, sto bene.*' He shrugs simply.

Campagna for Sardinians means 'the countryside', but is somehow not the same thing at all. This literal description is far too prosaic. *Campagna* is more an entity unto itself, a sort of Arcadia, a sort of Inferno at times (if there is rain, wind, insects, sickness). It is an all-absorbing place of both intense labour and acute pleasure. While many may 'retire' from their traditional jobs, no one ever 'retires' from *Campagna*, however much work and maintenance it may require. It is a love that lasts a lifetime. Mauro and his extended family have been going to *Campagna* at dawn and dusk, every single day, every day of their lives. 'Sundays didn't exist in my family,' he is fond of saying, 'We were up early and in *Campagna*, back in time for mass and then lunch, then back to *Campagna*.'

Campagna is not a place, it is a way of life.

Another day, after tending the vines, he shows me some photos of grape bunches he has taken on his phone. As he scrolls through them with a soil-crusted forefinger he mutters dreamily, almost imperceptibly, '*Ci sono certi momenti … .*' (There are certain moments … .)

He has a feeling towards *Campagna* that I can only describe as romantic. I look at his hands, black in their cracks and around the nails; his lower arms covered in welts from the insects that bite him as he prunes. A one-sided romance, perhaps, that requires constant dedication and often gives back only pain in return.

Mauro makes Vernaccia di Oristano, just as his father did before him, and his grandfather did before that, and his great grandfather did before that. Vernaccia di Oristano is named after its eponymous vine, which flourishes in the valley of the Tirso river; the region where we live, Baratili San Pietro, being one of the most important areas of cultivation and production. This vine produces grapes that are small, pale-green spheres that turn golden once ripe. They have a particularly high sugar content and a honey-like flavour. The grapes are harvested entirely by hand, by Mauro and any of us willing to help him, and then pressed in his small *cantina*, with its wonderfully evocative smell of wood, yeast and wine. The resulting juice is allowed to ferment in chestnut barrels (filled two-thirds full) for around 100 days. The barrels (which lie on the side with their holes pointing skywards, are corked with a single upright quince from *Campagna*, a detail unique to Mauro, which he says helps contribute yeasts (from the fluffy skin of the quince) and also adds a whisper of floral, quincey perfume. After the juice has fermented for around three months (the length of fermentation depends on the quantity of sugar in the grapes), a layer of yeasts forms on the surface of the wine, which is known as the *Flor*. *Vernaccia giovane*, or young Vernaccia, can now be decanted from the barrel and drunk as it is.

This young Vernaccia pairs particularly well with seafood, fish, bottarga, pasta dishes and most *antipasti*. It has a straw yellow hue and floral notes of asphodel and honeysuckle, and a slightly higher alcohol content than most white wines (around 15% average). It is much more fragrant and lasting on the palate than most white wines, a world away from the other main Sardinian white wine – a light, crisp and mineral-y Vermentino. It is the wine we drink with every meal in the family, as its stronger flavour means it can pair with pork and sausage as well as fish and vegetarian dishes.

Something extraordinary then begins to happen in those quiet barrels in Mauro's *cantina*, and over time the Vernaccia ages organically and changes its character completely. Mauro, when he explains this wine to people, says that he is just a conductor, and the grapes are what both do the work and produce the 'miracle', a testament to the idea that the high quality of the primary material is essential. In a way he is right, for in this extraordinary process of metamorphosis, where nothing is added or taken away, the grapes manage to undergo an evolution that is quite unique.

Il Flor

Derived from the Latin word for 'flower', this term is used to describe the yeasts that accumulate and form a veil over the Vernaccia as it begins to age. They bloom in circular cloudy clusters, and eventually form a unified wrinkled veil over the wine. Though the grapes must be just so, it is really the yeasts found in the skins of the grapes (and the atmosphere around them, and within the *cantina* and barrels) that are the true wonder, as they are extraordinary in their ability to adapt to their environment. Once they have metabolised all of the sugars in the wine they change their genetic make-up and begin to metabolise other substances, such as alcohol. These yeasts interact with the layer of oxygen above them in the semi-full barrels and form new chemical compounds and transform existing ones, producing the characteristic bouquet of an aged Vernaccia di Oristano.

Su Murruai

The bouquet, flavour, unique harmony, or characteristic taste and nature of Vernaccia di Oristano has its own name, *Su Murruai*. This means different things to different people, as is so often the way when we use a mere word to describe something indescribable. *Murruai* is derived from the Latin word linked to the Roman custom of scenting wine barrels with myrrh. According to Mauro, what it really describes is the exquisite balance that Vernaccia achieves between the almond and peach blossom fragrance of the wine (its floral perfumes) counteracted with the slight bitterness of herbs and spices, and the latent saltiness imbued by the Maestrale. A perfume and flavour that is both strong and elegant.

The flavour of an aged Vernaccia di Oristano, as this mystical *Murruai* suggests, is something that is hard to pinpoint exactly. It has been identified as having over 62 separate aromas, most of which are olfactory reflections of the terrain that nurtures it: the salty tang of the surrounding sea, the spice of *macchia* herbs, such as helychrisum, wild rosemary, mastic and fennel, and the woodiness of tobacco, cinnamon and walnut husk. The tiniest sip provides an extraordinary balance of all of these complex flavours, and stays on the tongue, in the mouth and mind, for many minutes after, which is why it is often referred to as a 'wine for meditation'.

A Wine that Speaks Sardo

Vernaccia is fondly and ironically known as the 'wine that speaks Sardo'. Exposure to fierce and diverse elements is unusual in viticulture, and this Vernaccia vine, like the Sardinian people, is notorious for its hardiness and ability to endure harsh conditions. Battered by the Maestrale, which gives its charismatic salty 'kiss', and able to withstand long dry periods, the vine and its wine are considered one of the most unusual and rare in the world. It is important to note that this same vine can produce a wine capable of ageing only in certain specific areas of the Sinis peninsula. Many wine-makers over the years have tried to produce the same wine (planting the same vine, and employing the same wine-making methods) in different places, and none have succeeded.

There is no denying that wine-making in Sardinia is an ancient art. Recent excavations of an area of the Sinis peninsula where we live unearthed grape pips from Vernaccia vines that date back to the early Bronze Age (in Sardinia, the Nuraghic Age). However the name, Vernaccia, is not unique, and is given to various other wines around Italy (hence the importance of adding *di Oristano*). Most likely derived from the Latin *vernaculum*, which simply means a 'local thing' of unknown specific origin, the Vernaccia di Oristano has become a symbol of Sardinian identity; a strong, individual and eccentric wine, which defies easy definition and laughs in the face of adversity.

Listening to Mauro speak about Vernaccia it is impossible not to fall a little in love with this unique and ancient wine. His own passion is contagious, and his devotion to the process is truly awe-inspiring. Rigorous in his maintenance, upkeep and final harvesting, if I feebly attempt to help either prune or pick he can spot my vine a mile away, and will invariably ask, 'Who touched this one?'

There is a love he has for his wine that is both fierce and fundamental, and this sheds light on the process behind the product, which renders something as simple as how it 'tastes' almost superficial. When something is made with so much devotion, dedication and precision, coupled with total humility (he flashes a goofy, embarrassed smile when anyone pays him compliments, before furrowing his brow and repeating his mantra: 'It is the grapes and the terrain that count'), it is hard not to let a little of its magic flow through your own veins.

Vernaccia, Honey and Saffron Poached Pears

Serves 6

6 small, slightly under-ripe pears	This produces lovely, fragrant amber pears that have a delicate flavour and decadent appearance.
juice of ½ lemon and a few strips of peel	Peel the pears and place them in a bowl of cold water into which you have squeezed the lemon juice. Set aside.
2 tablespoons mild honey	Place all the remaining ingredients into a wide, deep saucepan and
2 bay leaves	bring to a gentle simmer. Add the pears, then cover with a round piece
a few saffron threads	of baking paper (a cartouche). Simmer until the pears are just soft when pierced with a knife, 30-35 minutes.
100 g (3½ oz/scant ½ cup) sugar	
1 bottle of aged Vernaccia, or Muscat, or sherry	
a small glass of water	

Lazy Dark Chocolate, Pear and Almond Puff Pastry Pie

Sfogliatelle di Pera, Mandorla e Cioccolato Fondente

Serves 8–10

4–5 large ripe pears

2 x 230 g (8 oz) packs of store-bought puff pastry sheets (round)

100 g (3½ oz) dark chocolate

1 egg, beaten with 2 tablespoons sugar, to glaze

30 g (1 oz/scant ¼ cup) whole blanched almonds

icing (confectioners') sugar, for dusting

An invention of time-short Monica's, which I have tweaked a little, this involves store-bought puff pastry, which I am all-too-happy to endorse, as it is generally fairly good. This is possibly the laziest tart I know, but also very delicious, and it makes a very good breakfast, too, with a cappuccino. Serve with cream or coffee or both. It is not overly sweet, which is part of its charm.

Monica uses two round discs of pastry to make a large circular tart but you can make a rectangular one if you prefer, or individual oblongs, too, which are nice as single portions.

Preheat the oven to 190°C (375°F/gas 5).

Peel the pears, quarter and core them, then roughly slice and toss them directly onto one of the pastry sheets, leaving a border of about 2.5 cm (1 in). Break up the chocolate into small pieces and scatter evenly over the pears. Brush the pastry border with water and place over the other sheet of pastry as a lid, sealing the edges and curling them up to close, like a pasty. Cut a few slits in the top to let the steam escape, then brush with the beaten egg/sugar mixture. Scatter over the blanched almonds.

Bake for about 30 minutes until golden.

Sprinkle with plenty of icing sugar and eat warm or cold.

Saffron Buns

Makes 10 buns

For the leaven

150 ml (5 fl oz/scant ⅔ cup) milk

10 g (½ oz) fresh yeast

30 g (1 oz/4 teaspoons) honey

1 scant teaspoon saffron threads (a large pinch) soaked in 1 tablespoon boiling water for a few minutes (or ½ teaspoon powdered saffron)

60 g (2 oz/½ cup) plain (all-purpose) or '00' flour

For the final dough

100 g (3½ oz/generous ¾ cup) raisins/sultanas (golden raisins)/currants

zest and juice of 1 orange

400 g (14 oz/3⅓ cups) strong (bread) flour

100 g (3½ oz/generous ¾ cup) plain (all-purpose) or '00' flour

10 g (½ oz) salt

80 g (3 oz/⅓ cup) sugar

1 egg plus 1 egg yolk

70 ml (2½ fl oz/5 tablespoons) light olive/seed oil, plus extra for oiling

100 ml (3½ fl oz/scant ½ cup) water, at room temperature

To brush

milk

2 tablespoons runny honey (optional)

Saffron is the *fil rouge* that runs through my life, from my earliest and happiest food memories in Cornwall eating saffron buns and feeding them to estuary ducks, to my discovery of saffron as one of Sardinia's signature flavours. Supposedly introduced to both Cornwall and Sardinia by the Phoenicians, these buns are the best way to celebrate the honey-and-hay-scented spice, and can't fail to win over even saffron sceptics. Serve toasted or warm with plentiful butter.

For the leaven, warm the milk in a small saucepan or in the microwave, then set it aside until it is just blood temperature (tepid – not too hot to hold a finger in for an extended period of time). Mix the yeast, honey, saffron (either whole threads with their liquid or the powder) and flour with the warm milk in a small bowl and whisk until you have a smooth mixture. Cover with cling film (plastic wrap) and set aside for 30 minutes. You should see lots of tiny bubbles forming, which means the yeast is working.

Meanwhile, soak the dried fruit in the orange juice for 30 minutes, then drain.

In a large bowl, combine the flours and add the salt.

In a separate bowl, whisk together the sugar, whole egg and yolk, oil, orange zest and water.

Once the leaven is nice and bubbly, add it to the oil and egg mix, then mix the liquids into the flour. Add the soaked dried fruit and bring everything together, then remove from the bowl and knead on a lightly oiled surface (you can also do this whole process in a stand mixer). Knead for a few minutes until you have a smooth dough (the dough is quite sticky, so use a bread scraper if you have one, to help you knead it and then scrape up bits from the surface). Place the dough in a lightly oiled bowl and cover with cling film. Leave to rise in a warm place until doubled in size, at least 1½ hours (or overnight in the refrigerator).

Scrape the dough out of the bowl and using a knife/dough cutter to divide it into 100 g (3½ oz) pieces, oiling your scales if necessary. You should get about 10 pieces. Shape each piece into a neat round (there are good YouTube videos on how to do this), then place on a lined baking sheet, a few inches apart. Cover with an oiled plastic bag, making sure it does not touch the surface of the buns. Leave to prove in a warm place until doubled in size, at least 1½ hours.

Meanwhile, preheat the oven to 190°C (375°F/gas 5).

Remove the bag from the buns and brush them evenly but gently all over with a little milk. Bake for 12–15 minutes until they are golden brown and risen.

While they are still warm, brush the buns with the honey, if you like a sticky/shiny topping, or leave them as they are.

Autumn

201

Braised Sausage with Wine and Grapes

Serves 6–8

1 kg (2 lb 4 oz) good pork
sausage

olive oil (optional)

4–6 small clusters of grapes,
still attached to the stalk

2 small glasses of Vernaccia,
dry sherry or dry white wine

a pinch of fennel seeds/fronds
(optional) (you could also use
rosemary, if you prefer)

I buy sausage in Sardinia by the length, handmade by my local butcher
and his three strapping sons, who, when not hacking up meat, are to be
found extreme cycling in the hills around where we live, or getting their
hair/facial hair expertly barbered by my hairdresser. The sausage is made
in-house, and has salt, a little garlic, and chopped up fresh pork. Nothing
else. The father pulls out a length, coils it carefully into a perfect snail on
its crisp piece of paper and then wraps it up immaculately for me to take
home. The best way of all to cook it is on the barbecue. The second-best
way to cook it is like this. This is something we make when the Vernaccia
grapes are in season, around the middle to end of September; there is
something very satisfying about cooking the sausage in the Vernaccia
with Vernaccia grapes nestled all around it. Try to find some good grapes
still on the vine.

Serve with some simply boiled potatoes, mash or a green salad.

Choose a large, heavy-based frying pan (skillet) in which everything will
fit nicely. Set over a medium-high heat and begin to colour the sausage,
adding a little olive oil if necessary. Once the sausage has a good golden
colour on both sides, add the grapes to the pan and allow them to take
on a little colour before adding the wine (and aromatics/herbs, if using).
Turn down the heat and allow to simmer until the grapes are sagging, the
sausage is cooked, and you have a nice loose syrupy juice (you may need
to add a splash more wine or water during cooking).

Serve.

Braised Chicken with Grapes and Fennel

Serves 4

1 large chicken, jointed into 8 pieces (ask your butcher to do this if necessary)

1 celery stalk (optional, if making your own stock – see method)

2 carrots (optional, if making your own stock – see method)

3 tablespoons olive oil

3 garlic cloves, halved

a few sprigs of rosemary

1 large fennel bulb, cut into wedges

1 teaspoon fennel seeds

1 bunch of grapes

1 tablespoon sherry vinegar

2 small glasses white wine/ Vernaccia

1 teaspoon runny honey

1 tablespoon balsamic vinegar

about 100 ml (3½ fl oz/ scant ½ cup) chicken stock

salt

The meat is tender, juicy and falling off the bone, and the 'gravy' this produces has extraordinary depth. Winey, sweet and deeply satisfying, this is a perfect autumn dish.

If using a whole jointed chicken, you can boil the carcass with a celery stalk and carrots for a couple of hours to make a stock to use in the dish.

Preheat the oven to 190°C (375°F/gas 5).

Heat 2 tablespoons of the oil in a heavy casserole dish (Dutch oven). Season the chicken pieces all over with salt, then brown them, a few at a time, skin-side down, over a medium heat until golden brown. Turn them flesh-side down, add the garlic and rosemary to the casserole and cook until the garlic pieces just begin to colour. Once golden all over, remove the chicken pieces, rosemary and garlic and set aside on a plate.

Heat the final spoonful of oil in the casserole and cook the fennel wedges for a few minutes, allowing them to turn golden. Add the fennel seeds and grapes, then the sherry vinegar and wine, and allow to boil for a few minutes, stirring and scraping all the nice sticky golden bits from the bottom of the dish.

Add the chicken back in with its garlic and rosemary. Now add the honey, balsamic vinegar and a pinch of salt along with the stock. Place in the oven and cook for 40 minutes until the chicken is tender and falling off the bone. Taste and check for seasoning. If your sauce looks too liquid, remove the chicken pieces and reduce it for a minute or two on the hob until syrupy.

Serve with some steamed potatoes, mash or simply good bread and a bitter leaf salad.

WINTER

Inverno

Bitter Greens,
Beans and Blackbird Days

Winter in Sardinia is grey and artichoke-green, with flashes of fluorescent citrus. Bright baubles hanging over walls and in courtyards, trees laden with lemons and aching under oranges.

The season is a *sofferenza* that must simply be gotten through, looking towards the soft, supple promise of spring. Onomatopoeically brutal too, this Italian *inverno*, an echo of inferno, a burrow or dark place (the word derives from the Latin *hibernum*). We hibernate, like the tortoises, hidden under the leaves at the bottom of the garden, eating slowly and with purpose, bolstering against biting winds.

Cooking in this season I crave familiarity more than anything, the classic comforts of gratins and a little more meat than other seasons, because it feels substantial and satisfying.

Lorenzo witnesses his first English Christmas. He drinks his first English tea (with milk, from a pot) and my mum makes shepherd's pie, then hot mince pies with cold, thick cream. He sits with his dainty toes toasting in front of the fire. 'Yes,' he pronounces, unfurling himself like a cat, 'You English are good at *godendo* [really enjoying or making the most of] the winter. For us, it is simply something to be endured.'

Spring and summer are the Sardinian seasons that make sense. Winter is but a strange, short-lived necessity. Perhaps – I wonder - it is because it lasts so long in England that we know how to make the most of it. Our houses and our habits too; with carpets and wool and thick curtains, and tea, and baths, and hot wine and warm pies and toast and crumpets and things that drip butter, and marmalade-making and all the bits that make a winter bearable.

But back in Sardinia we, like the fruit trees, go into *letargo*. Once the olive harvest is over *Campagna* is quiet. The sheep are the only constants, looking shaggier than ever, their long-legged lambs tottering beside them. The fields too are in lethargy, green from the rains but fringed by the dark spiked shadows of leafless trees; the olives, stoical and silver, unchanged but now stripped of their shining fruit.

After *Ognissanti* the festivals gather speed. We emerge for feast days and festivals, Catholicism's cunning way of making a winter worth living; more frying, and more festive *dolci*. There is Christmas to cook for, the *Candelora*, the *Befana*, and *Carnevale*, then *San Valentino* too.

A passing phase, the Sardinian winter, a dormant state before the world wakes up again and life springs into action. We wait, almost patiently, and empty the cupboards. Cooking in winter can be a pleasure, because for once turning on the oven feels wise and welcome. Baking bread, if only for the smell of it cooking, is deeply satisfying – as is clearing out the pasta cupboard and making some reliable pasta dishes which involve very few fresh things at all. Reassurance in repetition and rhythm, rather than experiments and innovation. That can wait for the livelier months. Now we want our cheesy greens, beans and broths as we emerge, winking tortoise-like, from the weird incongruity of winter.

Spaghetti Puttanesca

Serves 2

200 g (7 oz) spaghetti

2 tablespoons olive oil

2 garlic cloves, sliced

a pinch of dried chilli (hot pepper) flakes

6 anchovy fillets

2 tablespoons unpitted green olives

1 tablespoon capers

100 ml (3½ fl oz/scant ½ cup) Vernaccia or white wine (or dry sherry or vermouth)

300 g (10½ oz) tinned tomatoes

a pinch of sugar/1 scant teaspoon light honey

a handful of parsley, chopped (optional)

salt

your best olive oil, to finish

A sort of Sardinian riff on the classic *puttanesca*, which (as the myth of origin would have it) involves nothing fresh, only what a Neopolitan lady-of-the-night may have had lying around her cupboards. This lady often has the end of a bottle of wine hanging about, and I love the background note it brings here, so I add it even if it's not necessarily traditional. I like to use a young Vernaccia, but whatever you have leftover will work. This is too good, however, to be just a fall-back dish. It is worth making even when your cupboards are *not* bare, and is one of my favourite pasta sauces: punchy, sweet, salty and satisfying. I love the sour saltiness of brined green olives here, but use what you like, as long as they are unpitted.

Put a large pan of well-salted water on to boil and cook your spaghetti until *al dente*.

Meanwhile, heat the oil in a sauté pan over a low heat. Add the sliced garlic and sauté until just turning golden, then add the chilli and anchovies and let them dissolve into the sauce, stirring. Next, add the olives, capers and wine, and simmer for 1–2 minutes before adding the tomatoes. Allow to simmer away for a good 10 minutes or so over a low heat, then taste for seasoning. It probably will not need any salt, but if it does, add a pinch. Depending on your tomatoes, this may be the moment when you want to add the sugar/honey if the flavour is still sour.

Lift the cooked spaghetti into the pan of sauce and add a slosh of cooking water. Turn up the heat and toss the pan a few times until the pasta is evenly coated and a nice sauce forms. Throw in the chopped parsley (if using). Serve with a drizzle of your best olive oil.

Cavolo Nero and Farro Sort-of Risotto

Serves 2–4

200 g (7 oz/generous 1 cup) farro

a few flavourings for the cooking water (a piece of celery stalk or onion, a garlic clove, a carrot, a tomato, a bay leaf, whatever herbs you have lying around)

extra virgin olive oil, for drizzling

2 tablespoons olive oil, for frying

1 garlic clove, bashed

5 anchovy fillets

1 head (bunch) cavolo nero

20 g (¾ oz) butter

about 2 tablespoons grated Parmesan

a squeeze of lemon juice

salt

This is one of my favourite ways to eat both cavolo nero and farro. We make it often at Spring and serve it alongside grilled lamb and grilled radicchio tossed in aged sweet balsamic. It has the most wonderful iron-rich depth of flavour and a delicious nuttiness from the farro. The colour too is reviving: a rich dark green, like a dragon's underbelly. It looks superbly life-giving, given its verdant colour. If you can't find cavolo, the beautiful Italian silver–black elongated cabbage that grows in the very depths of winter, then spinach is also delicious.

If you really are sure you hate anchovies, you can of course leave them out (and make this wholly vegetarian), but I think they are essential to the flavour of the dish and strongly urge you to try it with them in there.

In a saucepan, cover the farro by a few inches of water and add a few flavourings. Bring to the boil, then simmer for about 30 minutes until just tender (keep an eye on it and top up the water if necessary). Once happy with the consistency, drain and discard the bits of vegetables/herbs, etc. Season well with salt and your best olive oil and set aside. (This can be done in advance. The farro is also extremely good/useful in salads or warmed up in soups and so on.)

Heat the olive oil in a frying pan (skillet) over a medium heat, add the bashed garlic clove and cook until just beginning to sizzle, turn golden and smell good. Now discard it, and add the anchovies – they will hiss, stir and melt them in quickly, turning the heat down if necessary. Add the cavolo nero and a good splash of water, and sauté for around 6 minutes until completely wilted and tender. Blitz the whole lot in a strong blender with a splash more water to make a bright green, smooth purée.

Warm the farro with the purée, then add the butter and an extra glug of your best oil. Add the cheese and a squeeze of lemon juice and taste for seasoning, adding a little more salt if necessary, or a little more butter or cheese according to taste.

Serve as is, as a light-but-reviving winter supper/lunch, or use as a side dish alongside roasted/grilled lamb. It also goes very well alongside roasted pumpkin, or grilled radicchio tossed in balsamic. You could add a soft-boiled egg too … endless possibilities. If you want a quicker/more child-friendly variation, simply cook your favourite pasta and stir it through the sauce in the same manner.

Lemon and Wild Fennel Polpette

Serves 4–6 (makes about 30 mini meatballs, 18–20 larger/golf-ball-sized ones)

I make meatballs in midwinter, because we eat more meat in winter to bolster against the biting cold and because they feel suitably snowball shaped and hearty.

The last days of January in Sardinia are known as the days of the blackbird, and are supposedly the coldest of the year. However, there are tufts of spring sprouting courageously, the wild fennel that grows in the verges is rearing its delicate frilly head, and I pick some to lighten the intensely savoury flavour of these *polpette*. If you can't find wild fennel, by all means use some fennel seeds, which work very well. I also add lemon to lighten things up a bit and keep the flavour fresh.

Polpetta in Italian is also an endearment for a small child; a fact that brings me joy. 'My little meatball' is rather a wonderful nickname.

Meatballs are one of those things I was unjustly prejudiced against before moving to Italy. There is so much more to meatballs than the sad, solid little grey Flintstone boulders I grew up eating (maybe only at school too, because I'm not sure my mum has ever made a meatball in her life). The key to a good meatball is – perversely – the opposite of a good sausage. I like my sausages to be pure meat; pure, dark, chopped pork meat with a good distribution of fat and perhaps flavoured with fennel, garlic, salt and other spices, but no rusk or bread or anything else. Most Italian sausages I have come across are made this way. They are essentially like eating a minced pork chop with a few flavourings, whereas English sausages seem to be softer and more mealy, bulked out, stuffed and flavoured with bread, rusk, or whatever else.

While I mostly like my sausages meaty I prefer my *polpette* to be soft, giving, and not just about the meat. They should be flavoursome and moist, and almost melt-in-the-mouth. The first time I ate a meatball made in Italy I couldn't believe how good it was, not the hard, plimsoll-sole mince of my youth but soft, savoury and giving, juicy and delicately scented with herbs. There was so much more depth and flavour to it than the concrete-grey mince-y monotony I remembered. Apart from the herbs you choose to season the meat with here the other key ingredients are Parmesan and bread. Not only are these a genius way of making the meat go further, a true adherence to the *cucina povera* – old bread being the ultimate economy, a perfect way of 'filling out' food and using up something that would otherwise potentially be wasted – but the bread also makes the flavour softer, sweeter, more rounded. The texture it adds, too, is essential, making the balls when you bite into them soft and almost creamy, rather than grainy and chewy. The same is true of the Parmesan, it

Recipe continues overleaf

3–4 slices (about 100 g/3½ oz) stale bread, crusts removed

100 ml (3½ fl oz/scant ½ cup) milk

500 g (1 lb 2 oz) minced (ground) meat (I use a mix of pork and beef – make sure it has a good amount of fat)

1 large egg

4 heaped tablespoons grated Parmesan/pecorino

grated zest of 1 lemon

about 1 teaspoon salt

a good few sprigs of wild fennel, finely chopped, or a few crushed fennel seeds

a good grating of nutmeg

drizzle of olive oil (optional)

seasons the whole mixture and gives it a savoury and rounded depth, which the meat can sometimes lack.

If I buy mince, I always buy a mix of half pork and half beef, and I ask my butcher to mince it for me, and to choose pieces that have a good amount of fat on them. Mince shouldn't be too lean, ideally, as the fat adds flavour and succulence. Most mince here is a mix of pork and beef, the wise Sardinians know that the fat and flavour a bit of pig adds to the mix is indispensable. Minced beef, unless chopped through with lots of fat or even bone marrow, or cooked very rare, has the natural tendency to become hard, chewy and almost grainy.

When cooking your meatballs you can choose to bake them in the oven, or braise them in a casserole dish and add wine to deglaze.

Preheat the oven to 180°C (350°F/gas 4).

Soak the bread in the milk until it has absorbed all the liquid and is completely soft. Mush it up between your fingers, then add it to the minced meat in a mixing bowl. Add the egg, grated cheese, lemon zest, salt, chopped fennel (or seeds) and some grated nutmeg. Squidge everything together between your fingers until you have a smooth, even mixture. Shape into little balls (sized according to preference) and place on a baking tray (pan).

Bake in the oven for 25–35 minutes (depending on size). Break one open to see if they are cooked through.

Serve with a sauce of your choice (either *bianco* or *rosso* - see below).

In *padella*

If cooking on the hob you can start these in a frying pan (skillet) with a little oil and keep turning until they are cooked through.

In *bianco*

Heat a little olive oil in a heavy-based casserole dish (Dutch oven) and start to sauté the *polpette*. Cook over a medium heat until you have some golden crusts forming, turning with a fork occasionally and then pour over a couple of glasses of dry white wine. Leave to simmer for a minute as the wine evaporates, then cover with a lid and leave over a gentle heat for around 10–15 minutes until the balls are cooked through and the wine has reduced to a nice consistency. Eat, with abundant bread for mopping up juices.

In *rosso*

Alternatively, the meatballs can be served in a simple tomato sauce (see the variation on p.222).

see the variation on p.222

Winter

PERFECT ROAST CHICKEN

Two Ways with One Chicken

Just as every actor dreams of once playing Hamlet, so every cook dreams of writing – at least once – their own recipe for roast chicken. It is a rite of passage.

Roast chicken is one of the dishes I make the most often, something I crave constantly, and something that has popped up again and again, at relevant intervals, along the winding lawn of my life like a welcome and cheering molehill. It is a dish that tastes instantly of home, wherever that – or you – may be.

The birds of my youth were simply roasted, with thin, papery skin and lots of thick gravy, and most of all, great cumulus clouds of thick, lumpy bread sauce. My mum was not one for whizzing her bread into crumbs to make a smooth, refined and homogenous sauce; she shoved the slices in whole and bashed them up frantically with a wooden spoon, and the great uneven lumps of bread were part of its rustic charm. That was always how my mother prepared roast chicken, with boiled carrots, roast potatoes sodden in so much fat that it oozed through your teeth when you bit into them and

leeks in 'white sauce', just in case the bread sauce wasn't milky/creamy enough. This was Sunday roast at my house, and I feel as fluffy as mum's bread sauce just thinking about it.

The chickens of my present are a bit more Italian in their leanings, or a little more Sardinian perhaps. They are roasted simply, with lemon, maybe a little rosemary or garlic. Perhaps a splash of local dry white wine. Served simply as they are, with bread for mopping up the juices, or perhaps some potatoes, peeled and roasted in the pan alongside the chicken. Waxy, sweet and salty, and a whole world away from mum's fat-oozing ones. They are followed by a green salad, dressed sharply with more lemon and oil, or wine vinegar if lemons are not in season. This would probably be my last meal on Earth.

I buy a chicken once every two weeks, and it feeds us for the most part of a week. It is important to buy free-range, if your means allow it, because it will have a better flavour and also thicker skin, which is important for the roasting method, and makes for better, crunchier eating afterwards, too.

Marcella's Chicken with Two Lemons

Serves 6

This is an astonishing chicken recipe. It relies on no cheffy tricks but just one simple principle: that a chicken will cook evenly (thus avoiding dry breast and/or undercooked legs palaver) if rotated in the oven (beginning breast-side down to allow the legs to start cooking first and all the juices to run downwards towards the breast), and that a chicken, when its skin is intact and all of its orifices closed, will roast perfectly and juicily in its own sarcophagus of crispy skin.

This recipe demonstrates what a beautifully designed meat chicken is – it comes with its own casing. If you roast a chicken in the following way, you are essentially pressure-cooking the chicken flesh in its own skin (which will crisp up) while perfuming it delightfully with lemon from the inside out.

In terms of preparation it requires very little time or effort, but there is something especially pleasing (and perhaps perverse) about stuffing two little egg-like lemons back into the chicken's cavity and sewing/pinning its scraggy flaps of skin back up neatly, like a delicate surgeon, and finally tying its legs demurely together with ankles touching. Piercing the lemons too is an exercise in sensory pleasure, their electric scent shooting into the air with each puncture.

I have included a Marcella Hazan recipe in almost all of my books, and I see no reason to break with tradition here. She is a true heroine of the Italian kitchen, and I could read her as a novel. Her introduction to this recipe and written method is one of my favourites of all time. It is one of the most minimalistic recipes I have ever known, and one of the best. I was thrilled to discover she too roasts her chicken upside down, as I have been doing for years. Here is her description of the dish:

'If this were a still-life its title would be "Chicken with Two Lemons". That is all there is in it.

Again and again, over the years, I meet people who come up to me and say, "I have made your chicken with two lemons and it is the most amazingly simple recipe, the juiciest, best-tasting chicken I have ever had." And, you know, it is perfectly true.'

You will need toothpicks and/or string, and try VERY hard not to puncture the skin (in which case you will be rewarded with an extra-juicy chicken, which puffs up in the oven like a birthday balloon).

Recipe continues overleaf.

1 free-range chicken,
about 1.6 kg (3 lb 8 oz)

salt

2 medium lemons, or 1 large

Preheat the oven to 180°C (350°F/gas 4).

Dry the chicken well with paper towels and bring to room temperature. Season it well with salt all over. Pierce the lemons all over with a fork/ toothpick/tip of a sharp knife and stuff them inside the chicken's cavity. Close the cavity (pinning it with the toothpicks) and tie the legs together neatly with the string (not essential, but neat and tidy).

Place the chicken in a baking tray, breast-side down. Roast in the oven for 30 minutes, then rotate it so the breast faces upwards. Cook for another 30–35 minutes, then turn up the oven to 200°C (400°F/gas 6) and cook for a final 20 minutes or so until the skin on the breast is golden and puffed up. (Allow about 25 minutes cooking time in total per 500 g/1 lb 2 oz).

Allow to rest for a couple of minutes, then carve at the table, allowing the lemony juices from the cavity to run out, then spooning them over the carved meat. Eat with bread and salad.

Roast Chicken, My Way

Serves 4–6

1 free-range chicken,
about 1.6 kg (3 lb 8 oz)

a drizzle of extra virgin
olive oil

sea salt

a generous nut of butter,
softened

1 sprig of rosemary

1–2 garlic cloves

1 lemon, halved

a slosh of white wine

In terms of timing and rotation, my way of cooking this is similar to Marcella's (above); the initial roasting upside down to maintain a moist breast; the rotation and final flash of heat to crisp up and make golden the skin of the breast; but I sometimes like to add some fat to the chicken to help it along. Sardinian chickens can be a little lean, and I like a lot of juice at the end, which is extended if you add a little cooking fat at the beginning. The butter melts into the breast meat and the oil keeps the skin crispy and delicious.

I also like to add a little wine, to stretch the sauce even further, and I may add some other flavourings depending on what mood I am in. Here is the basic formula:

Preheat the oven to 180°C (350°F/gas 4).

Rub the chicken all over the outside with oil and then salt. Press the butter under the skin of the breast (without tearing it) so that it lies evenly between the flesh and skin. Place the rosemary, garlic and lemon halves inside the cavity.

Roast as above, beginning upside down and then rotating and turning the oven up, etc. Once the chicken is facing upwards again, pour a good slosh of wine into the roasting tin for the last 20–30 minutes of cooking.

Serve, with the pan juices drizzled over the carved meat.

Chicken Braised with Wine, Herbs and Olives

Serves 2

3 tablespoons extra virgin olive oil

4 free-range chicken legs/thighs/pieces (anything but breasts)

2 garlic cloves, halved

1 sprig of rosemary

a few sage leaves

a few sprigs of parsley (optional)

about 2 glasses of dry white wine

a generous handful of unpitted green olives (in brine)

1 tablespoon olive brine

salt, to taste

Variations of this dish are found throughout mainland Italy, often with the addition of tomatoes, onions and chilli, among other things. Commonly referred to as *pollo alla cacciatora*, which means 'hunter's chicken', it is a method of cooking also employed with rabbit. It is one of the nicest ways to cook both of these white meats, as it imbues their sweet and delicate flesh with a gamey depth and intensity of flavour, creating a wonderfully balanced and delicious contrast. Whatever the infinite variations, the core ingredients are indisputable: meat, rosemary, garlic, wine and olives. The hunter, of course, would provide the rabbit or bird, and probably the rosemary too, plucked from an obliging hedgerow on his way home from the hunt. The wine probably homemade, and olives fished from their homemade brine, where they had been floating in a large jar in the cool darkness of a dank cellar.

This version has no onions in the base, no carrots, no celery. The depth of flavour is instead provided by a few herbs, the intensely savoury flavour given by the browning of the meat (skin-on), the punch of garlic, the musk of reduced wine and the bitter-sweet saltiness of olives.

This is the kind of dish that you'll want to make in your favourite casserole dish or sauté pan; deep enough for sauce, wide enough for browning meat. The kind of pan/pot that only gets used for such braises, the kind of pan that travels happily from oven to table.

Note: This is not a precise recipe. You have to be a little open-minded about things, as it all depends on your chicken, your pot and your wine. Some chickens (normally battery ones) will release a lot of juice as they cook, some won't. Bear in mind that you'll need to adjust accordingly.

Heat the oil in a sauté pan (with a lid) over a medium heat. Add the chicken and garlic, and brown evenly all over. Keep an eye on both, keeping them moving so they don't become too brown. Aim for a nice, even, golden colour on both garlic and chicken. If the garlic becomes too brown, remove and add in again when you add the wine.

Meanwhile, finely chop the rosemary, sage and parsley (if using).

Once the chicken pieces are brown, add the chopped herbs to the pan and allow them to sizzle for a few minutes, stirring occasionally. Add the wine, allow it to simmer for a minute, then place the lid on the pan and turn the heat down to low. After 20 minutes, check the pan. If the liquid has reduced significantly, add a little more wine or a splash of water. Replace the lid and continue cooking for another 15-20 minutes.

Check the chicken is cooked through, it should be just falling away from the bone, and then remove the lid and add the olives and the brine (if your chicken is still not cooked, replace the lid and continue to cook for another 10 minutes before adding the olives). Reduce the liquid until you have a sticky gravy. Taste for seasoning, add salt if necessary, and serve.

This, like so many things, is even better the second day.

Winter

Ricotta Cloudballs

Makes 16 balls (serves 3–4)

For the balls

350 g (12 oz) ricotta (see Note)

1 egg

3 tablespoons fine dry breadcrumbs

2 tablespoons grated Parmesan

a few scrapes of lemon zest

a pinch of salt

a handful of chopped herbs of your choice (wild garlic, mint, parsley, basil)

For serving in simple tomato sauce

2 tablespoons extra virgin olive oil

1 garlic clove, bashed

a sprig or two of herbs of your choice (rosemary, sage or bay), fresh or dried

400 g (14 oz) tinned chopped tomatoes

salt, to taste

For serving in broth

600 ml (20 fl oz/2½ cups) chicken broth, seasoned to taste

wild fennel fronds, to serve (optional)

These non–meatballs, which I first tried in a little trattoria in Florence and took home with me to Sardinia, use fluffy ricotta to make them ethereally light and fresh tasting, and also vegetarian. I ate them served in a bright, fresh tomato sauce, which was smooth and velvety, and without the addition of extra cheese. They were perfect balls of happiness; simple, satisfying, and quick and easy to make.

They can also be served poached in a chicken broth (as pictured), or in a nice spring/summer vegetable *minestra*.

Blitz all the ingredients for the balls together in a food processor (or mix by hand). Leave for 30 minutes to firm up, then shape into 16 small balls. Place on a tray/large plate and set aside while you make your sauce or prepare your broth or soup.

To prepare the simple tomato sauce, heat the oil in a deep, wide casserole dish (Dutch oven) with a lid over a low heat, then add the garlic. Allow to sizzle and begin to smell good, then add the herbs, cook for a minute, then add the tomatoes, rinsing out the tin with some water and adding that too. Add a pinch of salt. Now start to add your balls, evenly spaced (they will swell a lot on cooking) and cover with the lid. Cook over a low heat for 15-20 minutes until the balls are swollen and plump and the sauce is nicely reduced. Taste for seasoning and serve.

If poaching in broth, add directly to the hot broth in a large, wide pan. Simmer over a low heat for 15-20 minutes until cooked through. Serve hot, garnished with a few fronds of wild fennel.

NOTE: This needs a good, stiff ricotta so that the mixture is firm enough to shape. If you buy supermarket tubs of ricotta (which is often more liquid), let it drain for an hour or two (or overnight) in a sieve (fine mesh strainer) lined with paper towels or muslin (cheesecloth) set over a bowl.

Blood Orange, Brown Butter and Honey Madeleines

Makes 20–24

140 g (4½ oz) butter, plus a little extra for greasing

100 g (3½ oz/generous ¾ cup) plain (all-purpose) flour, sifted, plus extra for dusting

3 eggs

100 g (3½ oz/scant ½ cup) sugar

2½ tablespoons honey

good pinch of salt

zest of 1 blood orange (save the juice for the icing, below)

40 g (1½ oz/generous ⅓ cup) ground almonds

For the icing (frosting)

2 tablespoons blood orange juice

140 g (4½ oz/generous 1 cup) icing (confectioners') sugar

dried rose petals, to decorate (optional)

You will need a madeleine tin (pan) or moulds

The madeleine is inescapably and quintessentially French, but it has also penetrated the Italian pastry canon, much like the macaroon/macaron.

When we chose the name James for our Anglo-Italian son, feeling Italian in my new-found love of saints, I set about researching his name-saint, whose symbol is a shell. It seemed fitting to make a shell-shaped sweet in his honour, and there is no better shell-shaped sweet than the madeleine. These little cakes are so easy to make, once you have the mould, and endlessly delicious to eat. They make wonderful gifts, and excellent party cakes, for any sort of celebration.

The original madeleine is flavoured only with butter and a little honey, but I have adapted them to include ground almonds (a nod to Sardinian almonds and also contributing moistness) and increased the honey content slightly, as well as adding my other favourite ingredient: blood orange. These madeleines are wonderfully fragrant, with toasty notes from the brown butter. The batter does need to rest, so start in the morning to bake for the evening, or make the day before and bake the next morning.

You can easily leave them un-iced and serve for breakfast or a simple *merenda* if you prefer. The icing is more celebratory.

Melt the butter in a small pan and use a little to paint your madeleine tin (pan) or moulds very well, using a pastry brush to ensure you get into all the creases. Now dust the tin/moulds lightly with flour and tap off any excess. Place in the refrigerator while you get on with the batter.

Using a stand or hand-held mixer, start whisking your eggs with the sugar.

Continue heating the butter. You want to caramelise it, which will take a good few minutes, but keep an eye on it so it doesn't catch. It will bubble and pop away happily and then you will start to smell the nutty scent as it turns just brown. Remove from the heat and add the honey, stirring to dissolve. Decant to help it cool down, then whisk in the salt and set aside.

Continue whisking the eggs and sugar until they triple in volume and become thick and mousse-like. Lifting the whisk and letting a trail fall, you should see it hold its shape easily. Fold in the cooled butter and honey mixture, then fold in the orange zest, sifted flour and ground almonds. Stir gently to combine, trying not to knock too much air out of the batter. Cover and rest in the refrigerator either for a couple of hours or overnight.

When ready to bake, preheat the oven to 190°C (375°F/gas 5).

Spoon the batter into the prepared tin/moulds, filling each shell only about two-thirds full. Bake for 12–15 minutes until golden.

Prise out and eat, preferably immediately, or ice them once they are cool.

Mix the icing ingredients to the right consistency (just dripping from the spoon) and then dunk the top half of each cake into the icing. Decorate each with a dried rose petal, if wished, and allow to dry on a baking rack.

Winter

Mandarin Curd Pavlova with Frosted Bay and Yoghurt Cream

Serves 8–10

For the meringue

½ teaspoon lemon juice

a pinch of salt

3 egg whites

175 g (6 oz/generous ¾ cup) granulated sugar

1 teaspoon cornflour (cornstarch)

a scrape of vanilla seeds/some vanilla paste/extract

For the cream

250 ml (8½ fl oz/1 cup) whipping cream

100 ml (3½ fl oz/scant ½ cup) thick Greek yoghurt

120 g (4 oz/1 cup) icing (confectioners') sugar, sifted, plus extra for dusting

finely grated zest of 1 mandarin/clementine

To finish

1 x jar Mandarin Curd (see p.228)

1 orange and 1 fresh mandarin/clementine, peeled and sliced/segmented

a handful of fresh bay leaves, washed and patted dry

Pavlova is often viewed as a summer dish, but can be equally delightful in winter. It is quick, instantly impressive and extremely versatile, and provides a becomingly fresh festive sweet treat to counteract all those darkly indulgent, sultrily boozy puddings.

There are several twists I use to make this version a little lighter than the standard pav: less sugar than traditional recipes, lemon in the meringue, a little tangy yoghurt in the cream and then the sharp curd on top.

In an ideal world you would make this pudding in January having already made your citrus curd to give as gifts over Christmas and this would use up that small jar left over, just in time for Epiphany. This makes the process extra quick: a pudding you can pull off in a late morning in time for lunch. However, there is of course nothing to stop you starting from scratch if you have not already made your curd (see p.228).

Preheat the oven to 150°C (300°F/gas 2). Line a baking sheet with baking paper.

For the meringue, place the lemon juice in a mixing bowl with the pinch of salt and the egg whites and begin to whisk. Beat the whites to stiff and shiny peaks, then beat in the sugar gradually, a little at a time, beating until you have soft peaks. Beat in the cornflour and the vanilla.

Spread the meringue evenly onto the lined baking sheet, creating a circle about 18-20 cm (7-8 in) across, flattening out the middle and raising the sides a little to allow space for the fruit/cream. Bake for around 1 hour until firm. Check underneath to see if it has set properly; the top should be crisp too. Turn the oven off and leave the pavlova to cool inside.

Remove the cooled pavlova from the oven and lift carefully off the baking sheet and onto a serving plate.

Whip the cream to stiff peaks, then fold through the yoghurt and the icing sugar, followed by the zest. Spread the cream over the base of the meringue, then swirl the mandarin curd over and decorate with slices/segments of citrus and the bay leaves. Dust with icing sugar and serve.

Mandarin Curd

Makes around 4 medium jars

6 or 7 mandarins

1 large lemon

3 eggs plus 5 egg yolks

a good pinch of salt

250 g (9 oz/generous 1 cup) sugar

200 g (7 oz) butter, cut into pieces

The word curd is a wonderful one; the gentle purring 'currr' a lulling lullaby as you curl into a soft buttery bed, only to be slapped awake by the sharp sting of citrus and the thud of the final 'd'.

Like so many things in life a good curd is about balance. Balance between thickness and dollop-ability, between sharpness and sweetness, between butter and eggs and enough citrus for all that fat not to overwhelm.

After discovering that I was now the proud owner of my own mandarin tree, the citrus curd of 2022 was mandarin. You can use other combinations of citrus as you please – a little lemon is always good for the essential tartness, but otherwise play around with grapefruit, blood orange and clementine.

Sterilise your jars (see p.169).

Zest and juice the fruit (you want 300 ml/10 fl oz/1¼ cups juice).

Mix the juice, zest, eggs and yolks, salt and sugar and place in a medium saucepan over a low heat. Whisk until the sugar has melted, then add half of the butter. Continue cooking and whisking over a medium heat until the butter has been incorporated, then add the rest of the butter and continue cooking and stirring for another 8–10 minutes until the mixture starts to bubble.

Strain through a sieve (fine mesh strainer) and decant into your prepared jars. Store in the refrigerator (this will keep for a good fortnight if unopened). It is a nice loose curd that can be drizzled when at room temperature, or spread when cold.

Mayonnaise

Makes a small bowl/jar

3 very fresh egg yolks

1 scant teaspoon sea salt

2 teaspoons lemon juice

1 teaspoon red wine vinegar

200 ml (7 fl oz/scant 1 cup)
your best olive oil

To think that it has taken me three books to write about mayonnaise!

Mayonnaise is not an Italian invention. In fact, there is much dispute as to where exactly it does come from, but it has been heartily embraced by Italians, mostly – it must be said – in the ready-made, squeezy-tubed variety available in supermarkets and employed in finger sandwiches of various descriptions (*tramezzini*). I eat it too with the boiled meat served after a *minestra*, which is a winning combination. Hot, savoury, poached meat and cold, peppery, sharp mayo is absolutely delicious.

When I make mayonnaise at home I use only the family's homemade extra virgin olive oil. The new oil, made from the olives gathered and pressed at the end of the year, has a flavour like artichokes and freshly cut grass. When a mayonnaise is made with this oil it becomes less something you spread unthinkingly in sandwiches or slather on burger buns, and instead becomes truly a meal in itself – something very special, the centrepiece of the table, around which you can build a meal. When you have an oil this good and flavoursome, the mayonnaise becomes simply a wobbling, creamy unguent of this oil, a way of celebrating its flavour, offset with a little salt and acid, in a thick and unctuous form. When making a mayonnaise with normal (less highly flavoured) oil – a more classically French sort of mayonnaise, I would add some mustard perhaps, for punch and extra flavour, but here the flavour of the oil is sufficiently forceful; to add mustard would be a crime. There is truly nothing better than this mayonnaise to eat with fresh crusty bread, with chips, with crispy-skinned roast chicken, with baked fish, with boiled new potatoes, with freshly cut tomatoes, with baby vegetables, fried artichokes, with fat chunks of tuna, boiled green beans, dolloped onto soup … .

I use a mixture of lemon juice and vinegar for acidity; I like the sprightly freshness of the lemon and the grounding punch of the vinegar.

Start whisking the egg yolks with the salt, lemon juice and vinegar, using either a hand-held whisk or a stand mixer, until creamy. Begin adding the oil, drop by drop or in a very fine drizzle. Keep mixing all the time, making sure the mixture doesn't split. Once thick and creamy, taste for seasoning, adding more acid or salt if necessary.

If the mayo splits while making, scrape out the split mixture, start again with a fresh yolk, and add the split mixture in drop by drop, mixing all the time until thick and creamy.

Endive and Speck Gratin

Serves 4–6

4 heads of endive

100 g (3½ oz) butter, plus an extra knob for the endive

olive oil (optional)

1 small glass of white wine

100 g (3½ oz/generous ¾ cup) plain (all-purpose) flour

800 ml (27 fl oz/generous 3 cups) whole milk

freshly grated nutmeg

8 slices of speck ham/pancetta/bacon

70 g (2½ oz) Parmesan (or cheese of your choice), grated

salt and pepper

If I were a vegetable, I could think of no better fate than being rolled snugly in ham, blanketed in béchamel and sprinkled with cheese, before being baked in a hot oven until crisp and golden.

The endive, that wonderfully useful, reliable and beautiful vegetable, is such a joy to have around in the depths of winter. It is refreshingly crisp, fresh and sweet, with the faintest bitter backdrop. I love to use it raw in salads but I also love to cook it.

Endives are part of the chicory family, and the simple chicory we know in England usually refers to the slim, elegant, closed-bud Belgian endive. This has conquered the world and chef's hearts everywhere, thanks to its elegant shape and delicate colouring and flavour. While I can easily get hold of them in Italy, they do not generally grow here in Sardinia, curlier types of chicory are more common, but I do love the Belgian for this particular recipe, as its neat shape works so well.

This is another adaptation of one of my grandmother's staple recipes; she made this often, and used English cooked ham and Cheddar cheese. It was a classic French recipe that she Anglicised, and now I have Italianised. She also boiled her endive while I braise mine, as I think the final flavour is better; I love the slight caramelisation.

This is a stand-alone main dish (alongside a green salad) or if you want to omit the speck and make it vegetarian that is delicious too. It also works very well next to roast chicken.

First, cook the endive. Slice it into halves lengthways, or quarters if the heads are very large. Warm the knob of butter in a sauté pan (with a lid) over a medium heat until it is foaming. Add the endive pieces so they fit snugly and cover the base of the pan. Sprinkle over some salt and cook, turning occasionally. The pieces should take on a nice even golden colour over 10 minutes or so. If things get too brown, add a little oil. Now pour in the glass of wine, place a lid over the pan and turn the heat down to low. Leave to cook for 10–15 minutes until the endive is just tender but still holding its shape.

Meanwhile, make your béchamel. Heat the 100 g (3½ oz) of butter in a pan until melted. Add the flour and stir, cooking for a few minutes until it smells of digestive biscuits. Add the milk, a little at a time, stirring well until you have a smooth sauce. Season with nutmeg and salt and pepper, to taste.

Preheat the oven to 180°C (350°F/gas 4).

Remove the endive from the heat. When cool enough to handle, wrap each piece in a slice of speck and lay them in a large gratin dish. Pour any endive cooking liquid into the béchamel and stir, then pour this over the endive. Sprinkle with the grated cheese and bake for 30–35 minutes until golden and bubbling.

Whole Mullet Baked in Salt

Serves 4

around 500 g (1 lb 2 oz) salt

1 whole grey mullet (about
1 kg/2 lb 4 oz), gutted but not
scaled (the scales help stick to
the salt and thus the skin peels
away more easily when serving)

bay leaves, rosemary, myrtle,
wild fennel, lemon slices or
herbs of your choice (optional)

your best olive oil, to serve

If there was a fish that symbolised Sardinia for me it would be the mullet. Perhaps surprising, as it is not a notable sea fish, a glamorously gleaming bream or silver shining sea bass, or something you would necessarily think of as particularly Mediterranean. However, in our region specifically, the mullet is a fundamental part of the food culture and prized for its eggs (which are salted and dried to make bottarga) and for its flavourful white flesh, which is eaten in an extraordinary variety of ways. Baked, boiled, braised, barbecued, there is no cooking method to which the mullet does not adapt itself, and while it may lack the delicacy of a sea bass it compensates in its versatility and flavour. Oilier, with a firm and nutty flesh, the mullet is particularly good barbecued, or cold in a sharp salad the next day (here with onions, tomatoes and basil is common, or with finely sliced celery).

Grey mullet, admittedly odd-looking fish with flat heads, pointed noses, weak chins and large doleful eyes, live in the brackish lakes around Cabras, a fishing village turned thriving tourist town nearby, famed for its bottarga production. I buy my mullet from the *consorzio* there, where they are fished fresh every morning. If you arrive after 8.30am you'll most likely walk away empty-handed. The boats are lined up outside, still shining with water, and the fishermen/shop assistants (one and the same) squelch around in wellies and waders as they wrap your wet fish in paper and plonk it unceremoniously into a plastic bag.

Baking a fish under salt in this way is incredibly simple and forgiving, and yields almost mythical results. The fish absorbs exactly as much salt as it needs, it is never too salty or underseasoned, it just *knows*. The texture of the flesh is tender and succulent, as you are essentially steaming the fish in a salty sarcophagus.

Preheat the oven to 190°C (375°F/gas 5).

Mix the salt in a bowl with enough water to get it to the consistency of damp sand (this helps it stick to the fish). Place half of the salt in the centre of a baking tray (pan) and place the fish on top of it. If using, stuff the cavity of the fish with the herbs of your choice and lemon slices. Cover the fish with the rest of the salt, pressing it down to form a nice white mound. There should be no part of the fish showing.

Bake in the oven for 25–30 minutes.

Remove and allow to rest for a few minutes before breaking the salt crust and peeling back the skin gently to reveal the flesh. Serve in pieces, if you like, or what I usually do is roughly loosen the fillets from the bones and then leave the whole thing on a serving platter in the centre of the table with a fish slice for people to help themselves. Drizzle with oil, to serve.

Winter

Squid Sauce with Squid Pasta

Totani in Umido con Calamarata

Serves 4

3 small/medium *totani* or squid

2–3 tablespoons extra virgin olive oil, plus extra to serve

a small pinch of dried chilli (hot pepper) flakes

1 garlic clove, halved

a few sprigs of wild fennel/ a small pinch of fennel seeds (optional)

a handful of chopped fresh flat-leaf parsley, plus extra to serve

a large glass of dry white wine

400 g (14 oz/generous 1½ cups) passata/fine tomato pulp

400 g (14 oz) *calamarata* pasta (or shape of your choice)

salt

It is common in Italy, and in our household especially, to serve seafood (specifically squid-based) pasta sauces with one of two pasta shapes: *paccheri* or *calamarata*.

Paccheri are great, sturdy tubes that are robust enough to hold their own next to a good thick seafood ragu, and also smooth and slippery so no ridges, twists or nubs get in the way of your slick, sweet sauce. Their stubbier sisters are *calamarata*, which are named after calamari, as they are thinner in width and look like rings of cut calamari or squid, specifically the type you might frequently find fried. I like *calamarata* with this dish, as it mirrors the rings of the *totani*, making it a sort of trick of the eye, impossible to tell what is fish and what pasta.

Totani are a new discovery to me, a member of the same family as squid (a cephalopod mollusc) they have slightly more elongated bodies and smaller, more arrow-shaped fins. When cooked they have a similar flavour, but a more compact, less chewy and pinker flesh. They are native to the Mediterranean and I can find them in the market during winter, making this the perfect winter supper pasta dish, perhaps as your Christmas eve *primo*, before a big roasted fish. This is one of Monica's celebratory recipes.

First, prepare your *totani*/squid. You can ask your fishmonger to do this for you, if you like, or do it yourself. You need to pull off the heads from the bodies, remove the quill (a thin, transparent backbone that runs down the top of the body) and discard it. Remove the innards from inside the body and discard. Then cut away the beak and eyes from the head section so that you are left with only the cleaned body tubes (wings still attached) and the tentacles. Cut the body tubes into rings about 2 cm (¾ in) wide, then set all your cleaned and prepped bits aside.

Heat the olive oil in a sauté pan (that has a lid) over a medium-low heat. Add the chilli, garlic and fennel (if using), and allow to sizzle and just begin to turn golden, then turn up the heat, add the *totani*/squid and parsley and sauté for a few minutes. Add the wine and allow to bubble away, then add the passata/tomatoes. Cover with the lid, turn the heat down to a simmer and leave to cook for 20–30 minutes until the *totani* pieces are tender. Taste the sauce and adjust for seasoning.

Meanwhile, cook your pasta in a large pan of salted boiling water until *al dente*.

Drain the pasta and add the *totani* and sauce to the pan. Stir and toss well over the heat for a few minutes.

Serve, adding a splash of extra virgin olive oil and a sprinkle of extra chopped parsley.

Porchetta

Serves 4–6

1 section of pork belly, ribs removed (about 800 g/ 1 lb 12 oz)

3 teaspoons sea salt

2 glasses of Vernaccia or dry white wine

honey (optional)

For the herb paste

finely grated zest of 1 lemon

1 teaspoon salt

a pinch of dried chilli (hot pepper) flakes

a handful of wild fennel or 2 teaspoons fennel seeds

2 or 3 sprigs of rosemary, leaves only

4 or so sage leaves

2 garlic cloves

Porchetta is traditionally a boned and stuffed whole roast young pig, roasted over a spit and served in slices, often between bread. It is a speciality of central Italy, although sold all over at fairs and festivals; the Italian equivalent of a hog roast. The Sardinian *porcheddu* or *maialetto* is similar, though usually specifically a suckling pig and especially loved here, forming the main course of most celebrations (Christmas, Sundays, weddings, etc.). The Sardinian version is left plain but served on myrtle leaves to perfume the meat; the central Italian recipe usually includes flavourings of fennel and garlic.

Wild fennel goes so well with anything piggy, and adds a lovely light lemony-aniseed note, which helps to temper the intensity. I cook and eat meat very rarely, and so when I do I want it to be really worth it, and I try to buy from the butcher and make sure it is local and outdoor-reared, because a pig's life is precious. I use belly because a) it is cheaper and b) it is fattier and thus more forgiving, the meat more tender than a loin. If you ask for a nice meaty piece of belly it needn't be overly fatty; it also depends on the breed. The lemon, also, is essential, though not always traditional.

I often serve this porchetta with some braised cannellini beans, cooked until creamy, which make a nice neutral foil for it, but the essential side dish is really a salad to cut through all the fat. Pork belly is deliciously fatty, but such obscene richness needs to be sliced with a seriously sharp salad. Choose a bitter leaf or a peppery one: rocket (arugula), chicory (endive) or watercress, or a mustard leaf, and dress it with plenty of lemon zest and juice, a drizzle of oil and a pinch of salt.

Buy the belly from your local friendly butcher and ask him to remove the ribs for you and score the skin well (either eat the ribs roasted or give them to your dog).

The night before you want to cook it, season the pork well with sea salt. You can be generous here as most of the salt will fall off. Rub it well with your hands, making sure the salt gets into all the cracks and crevices, and refrigerate.

Take the pork out of the refrigerator ideally an hour or two before you want to cook it, then dust off the excess salt and discard. Pat it dry with paper towels.

Preheat the oven to 130°C (250°F/gas ½).

Make the herb paste. If you like, you can throw everything in a processor and blitz it, but if you don't have a processor you can chop it all and mix by hand.

Turn the pork skin-side down and rub over the herb paste, then roll it up into a sausage as tightly as you can, skin-side out, and tie it up with string (there are good tutorials on how to do this neatly on YouTube, but even scruffily is fine, it is just important that it maintains its sausage shape). Place in a baking tray (pan) with fairly deep sides.

Cook in the oven for 3 hours until tender when pierced with a knife.

After this time, turn the oven heat right up to maximum, and continue cooking until the skin of the pork crackles and blisters (you can also do this under a hot grill/broiler, but you will have to keep a careful eye on it and rotate the pork with tongs to stop it burning).

Remove the meat from the tray and set aside, covered with foil to keep warm.

If there is a lot of fat in the tray, scoop some away with a spoon and discard. Pour the wine into the tray and heat it over a medium heat, stirring well until you have a deep-brown gravy. Cook for a good few minutes to boil off the alcohol, then taste and adjust for seasoning. You may like to add a little honey for sweetness, extra salt, water, or more wine, according to taste. I usually leave it as is. The meat is juicy enough to be good served alone, the juice is a bonus.

Gorgonzola Pâté with Walnuts

Serves 6

180 g (6½ oz) gorgonzola

150 g (5 oz) mascarpone

2 scant teaspoons brandy (you can use whisky, marsala or port, if you prefer, or leave it out altogether)

salt (optional)

To serve

walnuts

chicory (endive) leaves

Medjool dates

pears, sliced

crostini/breadsticks/crackers/bread

This is somewhat of a seventies dinner party classic, which has stood the test of time. Creamy, nutty and dangerously delicious, you will find yourself eating it by the spoonful, and it is literally the work of seconds. The contrast with fudgy dates and bitter chicory leaves is particularly wonderful (and beautiful to look at on a serving platter). Make sure to make a large batch and then use to dress pasta for the next day or two.

Whisk, blitz or blend the gorgonzola and mascarpone together with the brandy/booze of your choice. Taste for seasoning and add a pinch of salt, if you like.

Serve with some walnuts on top alongside the crudités in a dish of your choice, or chill overnight and serve the following day.

Golden Pear, Ginger and Vernaccia Christmas Cake

Serves 10

3 large pears

125 ml (4 fl oz/½ cup) aged Vernaccia (or Vin Santo/ Marsala or a medium sherry)

5 tablespoons syrup from a jar of candied ginger

175 g (6 oz) soft butter, plus extra for greasing

220 g (8 oz/1 cup) light Demerara sugar

3 large eggs

220 g (8 oz/2¼ cups) ground almonds

150 g (5 oz/1¼ cups) golden sultanas (golden raisins)

1 tablespoon candied ginger in syrup, roughly chopped

1 teaspoon vanilla extract

grated zest of 1 lemon

2 teaspoons ground ginger

½ teaspoon ground cinnamon

½ teaspoon ground nutmeg

a good pinch of salt

For the icing (frosting)

250 g (9 oz/1 generous cup) mascarpone

100 g (3½ oz/generous ⅓ cup) thick Greek yoghurt

finely grated zest of 1 lemon

a little vanilla extract

100 g (3½ oz/generous ¾ cup) icing (confectioners') sugar

I adore Christmas cooking. When I was young, one of my most coveted, crinkled cookbooks was *Nigella Christmas*, which my dad gave to me under the tree in my mid-teens. I think it is probably the only cookbook from which I have made nearly every recipe. The food in this book, and Christmas food in general, is the most wonderfully heady mixture of gauche, generous, exuberant, rich, excessive, colourful, whimsical, fragrant and luxurious. Christmas in England is sort of like the Italian Carnival; the world gone mad, excess and eccentricity encouraged, clamorous with bizarre names and foodstuffs; devils on horseback, pigs in blankets, a figgy pudding made with … prunes. Christmas food – love it or hate it – has infinite and undeniable charm.

Every year in England I would make a traditional Christmas cake, dense and dark, full of treacle and fruit and laced with brandy. After a heavy Christmas lunch it would be our teatime treat and usually the straw that broke the camel's back sending everyone off either to bed to sleep, or for a brisk walk to stomp off the indigestion. I still love that sort of cake, but this I dreamt up as something a little lighter and more in keeping with my Sardinian surroundings. Not light in the fat-free sense, necessarily, but something elegantly golden and glistening, rather than dark, mysterious and boozy. Something that doesn't need to be 'aged' either, like my Christmas cakes of yore, which I would feed daily with brandy for weeks, but instead can be made a few days before and decorated at the last moment. I remembered a golden fruitcake in my beloved Nigella book and I reworked it. The addition of poached pears is a bit more fiddly, but worth it for the dampness and flavour. And the creamy-but-light icing offsets the spicy warmth of the ginger and pear.

This is a fresher, zingier and brighter fruitcake, which still has all the luxury and sophistication of a classic Christmas cake but less of the stopping power. It keeps well too – I kept it for two weeks (well-wrapped and in Tupperware in a cool place) before we decorated and ate it. Afterwards you'll be lively enough to play some board games or hammer out a hymn rather than feeling the need to lie down.

First poach the pears. Peel, halve and submerge them in a saucepan beneath the Vernaccia/sherry and candied ginger syrup. Cook, partially covered, over a low heat until completely soft, then remove and set aside to cool. Continue to reduce the liquid in the pan until it is syrupy.

Once cool enough to handle, chop the pears (discarding any core, seeds and stems) into smallish chunks and set aside.

Preheat the oven to 170°C (325°F/gas 3). Grease and line the base and sides of a deep 20-cm (8-in) cake tin (pan) with baking paper.

In a mixing bowl, beat the butter with the sugar until fluffy and creamy. Add the eggs, one at a time, beating well after each addition. Now add

Ideas for decorating

frosted olive branches

lemon slices

candied pears

ginger in syrup

sugared rosemary

edible gold dust/glitter

all the other ingredients, including the chunked pears and any remaining poaching liquor. Mix well (don't worry if the mixture looks a bit ragged or split at this point, it will settle down in the oven).

Pour the batter into the prepared tin and bake for 1 hour until golden and just set. Remove from the oven and set aside to completely cool in the tin before removing.

To make the icing, beat the mascarpone until smooth, then add the yoghurt, lemon zest, vanilla and icing sugar. Beat again until smooth. Spread over the sides and top of the cake to create a smooth and even surface. Decorate as your heart desires, although a nice golden/gingery colour scheme is especially pleasing to mirror the interior of the cake.

VALENTINE'S DAY

Saint Valentine was, according to the most widely accepted legend, a third-century Roman saint who was imprisoned for continuing to conduct marriage ceremonies between soldiers and their sweethearts (it was thought by the then emperor, known as Claudius the Cruel, that love or marriage would distract his men from his extensive military campaigns, so he banned it). The priest's disobedience was discovered and he was imprisoned and sentenced to death. While in prison he fell in love with the jailor's daughter, and before being executed on 14th February he wrote her a love letter signed 'From Your Valentine'. As is so often the case with saints, there are many varying versions of the legend, but this is perhaps the most popular as it so neatly explains the Valentine-card-giving concept, and the association of the day with romantic love.

At the market, as mid-February approaches, a flurry of scarlet, crimson, flamingo and fuschia floods the stalls. In the UK, I remember forever preparing forced rhubarb; so impossibly, perfectly pink, best poached in perfect batons and bathed in pale-pink syrup. In Sardinia, it is blood oranges that take centre stage, by mid-February at their most crimson, perfect for vivid pink icings and cakes; and then the endless bitter leaves, radicchio, Treviso and tardivo. Then there is the first blossom of the year, too, and my favourite — almond blossom, the first sign that spring is truly coming, the bare black branches bursting into pink and white flower. Lorenzo picks a big spray of the blossom, and I use it to decorate sweet things; the blossom itself is edible too and has the most exquisite honeyed scent.

It would seem wrong not to make the most of the edible opportunities offered by San Valentino given the number of beautifully crimson foods seducing you to do so. Here are some of my favourite pink-themed foods, without the slightest touch of naffness.

A Quick Pickle

Makes 1 large jar

1 head of radicchio
or 1 cauliflower
or 2 courgettes (zucchini), etc.

For the pickling liquid

1 small tumbler of vinegar
(I use apple or white wine
or a mixture of both)

1 small tumbler of water

2 teaspoons salt

½ small tumbler of sugar

⅓ small tumbler of extra virgin
olive oil

Optional additions

bay leaves

chillies

a couple of sprigs of parsley or
wild fennel

some split spring onions
(scallions)

1–2 garlic cloves

This is so simple to make and is a lovely way to serve or preserve a glut of vegetables. I like fennel and courgettes (zucchini) best, but you can do it with peppers, cauliflower, cucumbers, onions, whatever takes your fancy. It is light and fresh and a lovely balance of sweet and sour, and the addition of a good olive oil adds another layer of flavour; a sort of simple *agrodolce*. I also like the pickled vegetables served just warm (especially the courgettes) as a side dish in summer.

Slice your chosen vegetables as you wish and then place in a large, clean preserving jar.

Bring the pickling liquid to the boil and stir to dissolve all the sugar. Pour over the sliced vegetables and seal the jars. Leave to cool and then use as you see fit. Store in the refrigerator for up to 2 weeks.

If you want to serve warm or at room temperature (I recommend this alongside good cheese too), place the vegetables in the pan of boiling pickle liquid, then leave to cool a little before serving, with an extra drizzle of your best oil on top.

Winter

Agrodolce Radicchio Salad with Sourdough Croutons, Sapa and Burrata

Serves 2

2 teaspoons red wine vinegar

2 teaspoons sapa

4 tablespoons extra virgin olive oil, plus extra for frying and drizzling

salt, to taste

2 heads of radicchio

1 x jar Agrodolce Radicchio (see A Quick Pickle, p.243)

about 200 g (7 oz) stale bread (2 rough slices), torn into small pieces

2 small balls of burrata

rocket (arugula) or other green leaves (optional)

a few parsley or mint leaves

Based on one of my favourite dishes from one of my favourite places to eat, The Towpath Café in London, this is one of the nicest ways to eat and use radicchio. I don't love all sweet-pickled vegetables, especially those involving cabbage, turnips or anything radish-y, as I tend to find them a bit too sulphurous, but more gentle vegetables like fennel, cucumbers, courgette (zucchini) and radicchio work beautifully (I also love pickled pumpkin but that's for another day).

The radicchio here is a perfect contrast of sweet and bitter and sour, and works so well when flooded with the blanketing cream of a burst burrata. The croutons give welcome crunch. A very seductive salad.

If you can't find *sapa* (grape molasses) you can use pomegranate molasses or an aged balsamic vinegar (in which case no need for the red wine vinegar).

Whisk the vinegar, sapa, oil and salt together and taste for seasoning, adjusting as you see fit.

Pull away the leaves from the fresh radicchio and dress them lightly with the dressing. Arrange them on a platter interspersed with the agrodolce radicchio.

Fry the breadcrumbs/croutons in a little olive oil until golden brown.

Place the burrata in the centre of the salad, scatter over the still-warm breadcrumbs and drizzle with a little extra virgin olive oil. Sprinkle with some extra green leaves and fresh herbs and serve.

Blood Orange Panna Cotta with Honey and Rosemary

Serves 4–6

juice of 2 blood oranges
(125 ml/4 fl oz/½ cup)

1 tablespoon sugar

1 leaf of gelatine (2 g)

For the panna cotta

200 ml (7 fl oz/scant 1 cup)
double (heavy) cream

50 ml (1¾ fl oz/3 tablespoons)
milk

30 g (1 oz/2 tablespoons) sugar

1 leaf of gelatine (2 g)

To serve

freshly sliced blood orange

a little honey

a sprig of rosemary

Dainty, fresh and aesthetically pleasing, the perfect winter–into–spring pudding. You don't need to be particularly skilled/technical here, just a bit organised with timings to set both the layers.

Add the blood orange juice to a small saucepan along with the tablespoon of sugar and bring to a simmer.

Meanwhile, soak the gelatine in a little cold water, allowing it to soften.

Add the softened gelatine leaf to the juice and stir well to dissolve. Strain through a sieve (fine mesh strainer) and divide equally between four small panna cotta moulds (about the size of an espresso cup). Place in the refrigerator to set for at least 2-3 hours until firm to the touch.

Once firm, make the panna cotta layer. Warm the cream, milk and sugar and bring just to a scald.

Meanwhile, soak the gelatine in a little cold water, allowing it to soften.

Add the softened gelatine leaf to the hot cream mixture and stir well to dissolve. Decant to help the mixture cool and leave somewhere cool until it is no warmer than blood temperature (otherwise it will melt the jelly layer).

Pour gently onto the chilled jelly and fill the moulds nearly to the rim. Place in the refrigerator to set for at least 3-4 hours.

To unmould, dip the moulds gently in a bowl of hot water for a minute, invert a plate on top and then turn out. Serve with some freshly sliced blood orange, and a little honey warmed in a pan with some rosemary.

POMPELMO

Grapefruit

The grapefruit is an accidental hybrid between a pomelo and a sweet orange, which throughout its chequered history has been both referred to as Paradise Citrus and Forbidden Fruit, and yet the only reputation that seems to have stuck, limpet-like, to its pitted skin is that of the infamous diet breakfast of the 1980s. Or, stranger still, as an exotic antipasto a decade or so earlier. I still remember my mother going through a half-a-grapefruit-for-breakfast-phase when I was little, though in her defence it wasn't purely for slimming purposes, but also because she loved them. I inherited that love from her, as a toddler being fed one or two of her segments sprinkled with teaspoons of sugar. I still adore grapefruit, and though I don't eat it often, whenever I find one in my local *ortofrutta* I can't help but buy it, but only after digging a fingernail into its skin and taking a deep, closed-eye sniff.

The *pompelmo* (grapefruit) grows well in Mediterranean citrus groves, and has made its way into popular Italian drinks, though it hails originally from the Bahamas. A 'Forbidden Fruit' was first documented in 1750 by Rev. Griffith Hughes who described it in his *Natural History of Barbados* (wonderful visions of the excited Welshman ripping open the golden fruit and tasting its bittersweet insides for the first time – he pronounced it 'even more delicious and delicate than an orange'). Later, in 1814, another naturalist coined the term 'grapefruit' for a similar citrus found in Jamaica (the name perhaps chosen due to the fruit's habit of growing in clusters like grapes). The grapefruit didn't receive official classification until the 1940s when it was given the name 'Citrus x Paradisi', the 'x' signifiying hybrid.

There was a time in England that half a grapefruit was considered a decidedly fancy starter. My grandmother often served it, on a rotation with half an avocado (perhaps filled with some prawns/shrimp in *marie rose*), or often simply a large slice of melon. Such fruits were still considered the height of luxury and sophistication, especially as the Second World War and its rationing were a not-too-distant memory. For my grandmother, throughout her life, these fruits were the very embodiment of exoticism and luxury. I shared her view. I remember reading *Decline and Fall* as a student and laughing for hours at the priest Mr Prendergast's ecstatic exclamation on receiving half a grapefruit as a starter in a 'fancy' local restaurant:

'What a large orange!' He exclaims. 'They do do things on a grand scale here!'

An eccentric history for an eccentric citrus, the grapefruit is highly undervalued in the kitchen. Their ruby-red insides are instantly cheering, as is their aroma, and they arrive just at the very darkest time of year. There is something wonderfully stimulating and revitalising about their sourness and bitterness, which I come to crave in dreary January when almost everything else I cook/eat seems to taste decidedly beany, creamy or cheesy. Citrus like this is life-giving, it revives in a way no other food does, injecting an electric dose of freshness and acidity into our bleak and dismal midwinter days. There is a – semi-ironic – theory in Italy that the people who love bitter flavours (black coffee, radicchio, citrus) are psychopaths, or at least sadomasochists, as they must enjoy pain. Bitterness – specifically the sour bitterness so particular to citrus – is less about pain and more about the exquisite pleasure of eating things that make one feel truly alive; all senses prickling, veins pulsing with luminous pink, orange or yellow acid, lips stinging, teeth tingling, eyes squinting, eliciting spontaneous sharp and sudden intakes of breath. No other food has such a visceral effect and for that alone I adore citrus.

Grapefruit has a bitter edge all its own, in some ways similar to a very good olive oil, an almost-spiciness; for that reason it goes brilliantly in both the following recipes, where it is balanced by fat (in cheese for the salad and creamy pistachios for the cake) and enhanced by a spicy, grassy olive oil.

Grapefruit, Celery and Ricotta Salata Salad

Serves 4 as a side, 2 as a main

2 grapefruits (white or ruby, both work)

1 large fresh head of celery, outer tougher stalks removed

a bunch of mint, leaves picked and very roughly chopped or left whole

juice of 1 lemon

a pinch of salt

a few glugs of extra virgin olive oil, plus extra to serve

a hunk of ricotta salata/other salted cheese

a handful of nuts of your choice

I love citrus salads, and grapefruit with its almost savoury spritzy bitterness works brilliantly paired with a firm, lemony and salty cheese like ricotta salata. Celery provides crunch and further savouriness with an earthy edge. Mint works so well with citrus and freshens the whole arrangement. I love some well-toasted hazelnuts here, but walnuts would also work. Something for a rare sunny lunch in January, that will make you feel instantly alive. It's important to try to find a happy head of celery, with a pale juicy heart and plenty of leaves.

I have also made this with feta and goats' cheese very successfully if you can't find ricotta salata.

Cut away all the peel and pith from the grapefruits, then slice as you wish (either in chunks, pinwheels or segments). Try to catch the juice to use in the dressing (I cut the fruit over a bowl).

Cut the celery into short lengths (including the leaves, which are delicious). Toss with the grapefruit pieces, then add the mint, some of the grapefruit juice, lemon juice, salt and olive oil. Taste for seasoning, adjusting as appropriate.

Crumble over the cheese or scatter over shavings, then scatter over the nuts. Serve, drizzled with extra oil.

CHI VA PIANO…

Mauro has a favourite saying: *Chi Va Piano, Va Sano e Lontano.*

It roughly translates as 'he who goes slowly, goes safely and far'. He is so fond of saying it, that it's enough for him to begin with the first three words and we know what is coming next. As easily applicable to safe driving as it is to a style of living, it contains that simple wisdom that is so particular to him.

Living in Sardinia has given me time: given me longer lunches, second afternoons, sleepy summer days that feel like decades. It has given me a concept of 'island time', a lack of fret or hurry, which is at first frustrating, but then – *piano piano* – washes over you like a warm summer wave. You resign yourself to the greater external force and let yourself float atop the ocean of uncertainty and bask in eternal afternoons. After all, there is always *domani* (tomorrow).

This slowness, the infamous and soporific '*piano piano*', is neither lazy nor negative, quite the reverse. Like the apocryphal tortoise versus the hare, it is steady, sedate and dogged. It is not about shirking work or sleeping all day, but about making the most of the important moments with those you love, eating around a table, and then working steadily and slowly too, but never to such an extent that you make yourself unhappy or – most importantly – skip a meal. If I ever try to skip a meal 'to get things done' I am met with faces of abject horror from my Sardinian family. Working is essential, of course, but so is eating lunch. Most of the Sardinians I know work their whole lives, perhaps not in an office but in their gardens or plots of land (*ortos*), and the idea of 'giving up' such work would be totally alien. Why would you give up something you love?

This attitude to life, and approach to both work and the time spent away from it, is often attributed as the main reason Sardinians live such long lives. A focus on (specifically) outdoor work, steady but slow, on community and family, is what the experts believe provides Sardinia with a record number of centenarians.

'You see,' winks Mauro, '*Chi va piano …* .'

Pink Grapefruit, Pistachio and Polenta Cake

Makes a 20 cm (8 in) cake

butter, for greasing

120 g (4 oz/generous ¾ cup) shelled unsalted pistachios, plus an extra handful, roughly chopped, to decorate

80 g (3 oz/1¼ cups) polenta (cornmeal)

finely grated zest of 1 large pink grapefruit (use the juice below)

a pinch of salt

2 teaspoons baking powder

4 eggs

180 g (6½ oz/generous ¾ cup) sugar

180 ml (6 fl oz/¾ cup) olive oil

rosebuds/petals, to decorate (optional)

For the syrup

2 tablespoons honey (a light floral one to let the flavour of the grapefruit shine)

juice of 1 large pink grapefruit

A surprising cake this, a version of which I first tried in Oxfordshire at a lovely little tumble-down kitchen garden café called Worton. It was impossibly moist, a sort of appealing pale pond-green, with a lovely crunchy texture due to the polenta (cornmeal) and a surprising almost-spiciness from the olive oil and grapefruit. I can never resist alliterative recipes.

Serve with some yoghurt for a refreshingly zingy January breakfast, or with Earl Grey for a fragrant, citrussy tea.

It is also – miraculously – gluten and dairy free. At the café where I tried it they perfumed the syrup with a sprig of rosemary, which you could do if you like, but I keep it without. Another nice addition is a little ground cardamom, though not strictly Italian.

Preheat the oven to 180°C (350°F/gas 4). Grease and line a 20 cm (8 in) cake tin (pan) with baking paper.

Blitz the pistachios in a food processor until they form a fine, sandy rubble. Tip into a mixing bowl, then mix in the polenta, grapefruit zest, salt and baking powder.

In a separate bowl, whisk the eggs with the sugar and olive oil. Whisk the dry ingredients into the wet and pour into your prepared cake tin.

Bake for 40-50 minutes until just set and golden on top.

Remove from the oven and set aside as you make the syrup. Melt the honey over a low heat until liquid and just bubbling, then add the fresh grapefruit juice. Allow to simmer for a minute and then pour over the still-warm cake, little by little, waiting for it to be absorbed.

Decorate with roughly chopped pistachios and rosebuds or petals, if you wish. Serve warm or cold. This cakes keeps well for several days.

WAYS AND BEANS

Beans in my family came either in tins or on toast, and were rare. My father had a secret love of either eating them straight from the tin or pouring them – gloopy and cold – over his chopped iceberg salad. I never shared his love of Heinz, always thinking they tasted – cold especially – like a sort of oddly vegetal jam, so sweet and suspiciously shiny. There is an apocryphal story in our family that my uncle, after trying his first Heinz baked bean at school (my grandmother refused to buy them on principle, believing them to be the work of The Devil) wrote a letter home to his mother, with the unforgettable phrase, 'for lunch we had peas, orange with disgust'. This became our family's way of referring to beans.

When I worked in kitchens I came to know and love beans. Not of the infamous tinned and baked variety but instead braised, the Italian way, with some herbs and aromatics, then served simply perhaps alongside a steak and some *salsa verde*, or braised pork shoulder, or soupy under a leg of well-roasted chicken, or piled onto grilled bruschetta and doused in good olive oil. As I probed deeper into the leguminous world, I even became obsessed with a special Breton bean with a fittingly sing-song name, Coco de Paimpol, which have their own protected designation of origin. In the kitchen I spent hours coaxing the creamy best from cannellini, and lovingly braising borlotti in the oven, submerged under a shining film of extra virgin olive oil.

Then, when I finally moved to Italy, and more specifically to Sardinia, my appreciation for beans deepened further still, and I came to see (and eat them) as a dish in themselves, not just as a side or accompaniment. Here beans are eaten as a *primo*, instead of pasta, and seeing as these days we don't eat very much meat, there is often no *secondo* to follow, so we really just eat beans. Glamorous they are not, but they are reassuringly wholesome; good for you, cheap, nutritious, filling and delicious,

and a complete meal in themselves. For centuries whole civilisations have survived on a diet based around beans and yet they inspire unjustifiably mediocre reactions; Lorenzo, who has an irritating bean bigotry, always rolls his eyes when I tell him it's *fagioli* for supper, and then he eats three large plates-full, and I soak another packet, triumphant. He claims growing up eating beans was a penance, because they were always boring and just beans, but when you add all of the important things as described below, he says eating them is a pleasure.

There is something incredibly restorative in a plate of beans, something primitively simple and satisfying. Beans need never be repetitive or dull. There are numerous varieties, each of which has a specific flavour and texture, and the ways of cooking them differ hugely too. I have worked with chefs who like their beans with bite. I don't. Perhaps if serving cold in a salad I cook them a little less, to hold their shape. Otherwise I prefer them in a state of creamy collapse, when around a third of them have melted into the cooking liquid to create the most earthy, sweet, nutty, matte liquor anyone could ever dream of creating by human hand. Bean juice is manna from heaven, and the bit I eat first, savouring and sucking it hungrily from my spoon, returning to the solid mass of beans later, perhaps with grilled bread and some cheese.

When I say a plate of beans, I think this should be treated as a base, to which you can add and take away as you see fit. A plate of well-cooked beans is something I often crave, no embellishments other than a drizzle of the new season's olive oil, but then there are other occasions when you can add a little variety and throw in some peas, some pasta (small soup pasta), some greens, top them with pesto, ricotta, a herb oil, grated bottarga, chopped fresh tomatoes and basil, rocket (arugula) and lemon, tuna, a tangle of salad, or tuck them alongside a sausage or steak if you need something meatier and more bolstering. Any which way they are cooked and served, beans are the life-blood of my winter repertoire, and something that touch a particularly tender and primordial place inside us on a dark and drizzly December night.

Once removed from their pods and dried, some care and attention are necessary to release all that creamy, deep flavour from inside a bean's sun-hardened jacket. They must be cooked with care to achieve the flavourful heights they deserve.

If you are lucky enough to get fresh beans, that is another story altogether. Fresh beans can be cooked in all the same ways, but need to be cooked for much less time, and will have a creamier texture and a fresher more vibrant flavour.

GOOD FLAVOURINGS FOR BEANS

Do not simply boil beans in water. Beans should never be 'boiled' but rather braised, cooked in a little liquid, just enough to create a good amount of sauce and prevent them from catching on the base of the pan, but not so much that they are swimming. This liquid should be flavoured as you see fit. I usually add:

- a sprig of sage (especially good with borlotti and cannellini)
- a fresh tomato or two (or sun-dried in winter)
- some sprigs of fresh parsley
- a clove or two of garlic
- a small sprig of rosemary
- a bay leaf (more often with borlotti)
- a little dried chilli (whole or flakes)
- a peeled potato (this purportedly aids the digestion by absorbing some of the beans' sugars, which can cause flatulence, but I just like to eat the creamy, beany potato after cooking)
- meat (pancetta, a piece of pig skin – the traditional bean cooking accompaniment known as *cotena*, bacon, a chunk of guanciale; all of these things add flavour, depth and savouriness to your beans; they also add essential fat – all beans should have at least a little meat in them, according to Lorenzo)

I then add a good glug of extra virgin olive oil and sometimes a splash of red wine vinegar, depending on what I want the end result to taste like.

Cook them slowly, check the liquid and keep checking the texture until they are cooked to your liking. Set aside and then eat as they are, with good oil or in any of the following recipes.

For fresh borlotti, if you are lucky enough to get your hands on them, I often bake them in a 190°C (375°F/gas 5) oven, covered with liquid and the suggested aromatics in a deep roasting dish covered with foil, for about an hour until tender. Taste for seasoning and then season with more good oil, salt and a splash more vinegar to taste.

For dried beans – most specifically borlotti and cannellini, which are the two I use the most, soak them in lots of cold water overnight and then try cooking them in any of the following ways.

It is important to remember that bean cookery is not a precise art, as not all beans were made equal. There are some that will take double the amount of time to cook as others, all dependent on how and when they were picked and dried and packaged, etc. Keep checking and tasting and feel your way.

Braised Beans and Greens

Serves 4

1 onion, finely chopped

3 garlic cloves, sliced

4 tablespoons olive oil, plus extra to serve

4 anchovy fillets

3 sun-dried tomatoes

1 dried chilli or a pinch of dried chilli (hot pepper) flakes

1 sprig of rosemary

1 bay leaf

250 g (9 oz) dried cannellini beans, soaked overnight

enough water/stock, to cover

½ head of escarole, or bitter greens of your choice, washed and roughly chopped

salt, to taste

grated Parmesan, to serve

I cannot resist a rhyming recipe any more than I can resist an alliterative one, but this is a staple that I fall back on again and again throughout the winter, and something that gives immense sensory and nutritive pleasure. The only real recipe you need is how to cook the beans, the rest you simply wilt in the pan with a little oil, garlic and a splash of water until just tender, and then serve spritzed with a little lemon zest and juice, and drizzled with some more oil.

The greens are most often bitter, as they tend to be during Italian winter, and more often than not some kind of chicory or endive, or wilted cabbage or spinach.

For the beans, I like to cook cannellini for this, especially as I love the white contrast against the lush green. I sometimes melt a few anchovies in at the beginning, too.

In a deep saucepan, sauté the onion and garlic in the olive oil until soft and translucent. Add the anchovies, sun-dried tomatoes, dried chilli (if using) and herbs, and continue to cook for a few minutes.

Add the beans (drained) and enough fresh water to come to 10 cm (4 in) above the level of the beans. If you have stock (lucky!) then use it instead. Cook, covered, over a low heat for 1½–2 hours until the beans are tender.

Add the escarole, or chosen greens, and cook for 10 minutes more. Season with salt, a good glug of your punchiest olive oil, and some chilli flakes (if using). Serve, with grated Parmesan on top.

Another way to braise cannellini

If you wish to omit the step of chopping the onion and sweating it, etc., you can still produce excellent beans by placing everything in a pot (onion simply halved, rather than diced; garlic peeled), then cooking them low and slow until creamy. Season well with salt and some more oil before using as you see fit.

Pasta e Fagioli

Serves 4–6

For the beans

2 tablespoons olive oil, plus extra as needed

1 onion, finely diced

1 garlic clove, finely sliced

1 celery stalk, finely chopped (leaves are good too)

a few whole parsley stalks (finely chopped)

1 bay leaf

a few leaves of fresh sage (optional)

a small sprig of rosemary

1 dried chilli or a pinch of dried chilli (hot pepper) flakes

1 small hunk of pancetta, diced

2 sun-dried tomatoes or a squeeze of tomato purée

200 g (7 oz) borlotti beans, soaked in cold water overnight

around 1.2 litres (40 fl oz/ 4¾ cups) water

salt

For the pasta

2 tablespoons *ditalini* per person (and one for the pot)

extra virgin olive oil, to serve

A hearty and humble plate that pops up all over Italy, the first time I tried this it was made by Luca's mother in her pressure cooker, and I thought it was one of the most delicious things I had ever eaten. Sweet but intensely savoury and satisfying, it was a beautiful taupe plateful of soft, giving, creamy-bean textures, interspersed with the occasional pebble of *al dente* pasta. What a genius way to make the most of the bean juice, by poaching pasta in it and creating the most wholesome and earthy soup anyone could imagine. This is the sort of food legions could go conquering on, should circumstances require it.

The best thing to do is to make a big batch of beans, then cook the pasta in them last minute when you want to eat them. That way you can eke out the pot, and maybe put them to different uses too. The pasta is much nicer if cooked fresh and *al dente*, so portion out your beans and then add your pasta according to who's eating. I add a little pancetta, in honour of Franca who taught me to make it, and I do think the smoky depth here is very welcome, but you can keep things vegetarian if you like. I also do a soffrito first, which helps impart even more flavour to the beans, rather than braising them directly in water and flavourings.

The pasta shape I like in this – out of loyalty to Franca – is *ditalini*, a small stubbily short tube with great bite, but you can of course choose as you wish.

First cook the beans. In a deep, heavy-based saucepan, warm the oil over a low heat, then sweat the onion, garlic, celery, parsley, bay leaf, sage, rosemary and chilli until softened and translucent. Now add the pancetta and cook for another few minutes until everything just begins to take on colour. Add the tomatoes/purée, the beans, the water and another good glug of olive oil, and cook over a low heat for up to 2 hours until the beans are completely soft and collapsing.

When ready to serve, taste for seasoning and check there is enough liquid to cook your pasta in. Portion out as many beans (with their juice) as you want to serve and for each portion add 2 tablespoons of pasta, then 1 tablespoon for the pot. Cook over a low heat, adding a little more water if necessary, until the pasta is just *al dente* (around 6 minutes). Taste again and add salt if necessary, then serve with a drizzle of extra virgin olive oil on top.

Beans Terence Hill

Serves 4–6

2 tablespoons olive oil, plus extra to finish (optional)

2 garlic cloves, sliced

1 white onion, finely diced

1 bay leaf

1 small red chilli or a good pinch of chilli (hot pepper) flakes

250 g (9 oz) sausagemeat

a glass of white wine

200 g (7 oz) borlotti or cannellini beans, soaked overnight

1 tablespoon tomato purée

400 g (14 oz) fresh or tinned chopped tomatoes

around 1 litre (34 fl oz/4 cups) water

a little aged balsamic or red wine vinegar

1 teaspoon or so of honey

salt, to taste

grated cheese, to serve (optional)

It is funny the things that cross the oceans and are embraced into the communal cultural bosom and what falls by the wayside. Some predictable – Disney films jumped the divide, and are often even more droll when voiced in Italian (*Sword in the Stone*, an old favourite, is excellent in Italian). James Bond has been heartily assimilated by most Sardinians that I know, as have the Beatles, the Queen and Harry Potter. Some more unlikely things, too, seem to have made their way onto the Sardinian cultural landscape, dotted about like fluffily incongruous sheep.

La Signora in Giallo, or *Murder She Wrote*, provided the backdrop to every lunch in Luca's house, featuring the vividly attired Angela Lansbury with her unique expression that blended perplexity with cunning, would play through every mealtime, so that it almost didn't feel like lunch unless her incredulous eyes gawked at me from the screen as I ate my pasta.

Another film, which I have never known a Sardinian not adore, is *They Call Me Trinity*, which I had never heard of before moving to Italy, only to have my ignorance met by open-mouthed incredulity every time I ate a plate of tomato and sausage braised beans.

They Call Me Trinity, a spaghetti western made in 1970 and starring the blue-eyed, Venetian-born Terence Hill (true name Mario Girotti) is a ludicrous but lovable Italian-made Western, which became a national and international hit, causing a dish to be named after it. There is an infamous scene in the film where Trinity (Terence Hill) stops at an inn to eat, where a grubby innkeeper with a dour face and drooping moustache serves him a plate of braised beans. Trinity grabs the full saucepan, tells him to leave it, and proceeds to eat his way through the entire thing, accompanied by a whole loaf of bread, the last torn hunk of which he employs to perform an exemplary *scarpetta* (proving – if you were in any doubt – that this film was made by Italians). One of the most famous scenes in the film, it is perhaps no surprise that there are specific beans named after it, spiced with chilli, braised in tomato and enriched with white wine and sausage. You can choose to use whichever beans you fancy, or simply open a can. I tend to opt for borlotti or cannellini. Eat with bread and Trinity-like gusto.

Heat the oil in a deep pan over a medium-low heat and sweat the garlic and onion. Add the bay leaf and chilli, then the sausagemeat, allowing it to just take on some colour and stirring all the time to prevent it sticking. De-glaze the pan with the wine, then add the beans, tomato puree, chopped tomatoes and water (the liquid should come about 5-7.5 cm/2-3 in above the solids). Braise over a low heat until the beans are soft and the liquid is nicely thick, about 1½ hours.

Taste and check for seasoning, adding a little vinegar and/or honey if it needs a little acidity or sweetness (this will depend on your tomatoes and how flavoursome your sausage is). Add salt to preference. Serve with a drizzle of olive oil or some grated cheese.

LA SCARPETTA

Washing-up and a Philisophy for Life

No one ever writes about washing-up. There are, of course, many daily experiences that are perhaps best not written about, but I feel it is deeply unfair to banish dirty dishes to such dismal territory.

Anyone who cooks must deal with the dishes. And there is one fact about life in Italy that makes this often irksome task much easier and more appealing, and that is the *scarpetta*.

The *scarpetta* is just another example of the Italian gift for turning something (specifically food-related) seemingly banal into something whimsical with just the slightest fried-garlic whiff of romance. *Scarpa* in Italian means 'shoe', and *la scarpetta* means 'a little shoe'. In an edible context it is a way of describing the small, slightly shoe-shaped crust of bread you use to mop up the last sops of sauce from a plate. This little bread shoe has a devoted following among many Italians, for whom a meal is not complete without bread, the original companion. (The word companion itself derives from the Latin *com* or 'with', and *panis*, 'bread'). Lorenzo and Mauro are both of this mindset, and a meal without bread for them is not a meal. When something (a sauce, dressing, liquid egg yolk or soup) is especially good, Lorenzo will do his *scarpetta* at the end of the meal with great precision and deliberation, leaving no drop of sauce un-scooped, and then pass it, smiling, to me to eat; the ultimate act of love.

Gillian Riley writes about the Italian attitude to bread:

'No messing about with special knives and plates and bits of butter; bread is balanced on the edge of the plate it accompanies, or sits in fragments on the tablecloth, at hand's reach, to guide food onto the questing fork, mop up juices, enjoy on its own between bites, and be dunked in broth.'

Bread is served and eaten without ceremony or frippery; a true simple, solid staple rather than a dinky little dinner roll. It is scattered about the table, directly on the tablecloth and torn at will. Then, as plate/bowl of broth, pasta or meat are finished, the final little crust, shoe-shaped, scrapes the plate clean with crusty pointed accuracy.

The *scarpetta* is the perfect example of that peculiarly Italian blend of economy, pragmatism and romance when it comes to edibles. It means less washing-up (a fact Lorenzo is always keen to point out to me), it means less waste, and it also exhibits the kind of savouring and appreciation that is fundamental to the enjoyment of every meal in Italy.

Whenever I think of the *scarpetta*, it makes me think of a sketch from *Beyond the Fringe*, which my father used to recite over and over again. Alan Bennett, playing a vicar, gives a sermon about the meaning of life, in which he compares it to a tin of sardines:

'You know, Life-Life, it's rather like opening a tin of sardines. We are all of us looking for the key. Some of us—some of us think we've found the key, don't we? We roll back the lid of the sardine tin of Life, we reveal the sardines, the riches of Life therein, and we get them out, we enjoy them. But, you know, there's always a little piece in the corner that you can't get out. I wonder—I wonder, is there a little piece in the corner of your life? I know there is in mine.'

The *scarpetta* is the perfect Italian way of getting that last bit out of the corner of life, of scraping the bottom of the barrel of simple everyday bliss, of deliberately and doggedly delighting in that last morsel (and, meanwhile, saving on the washing-up).

INDEX

ACKNOWLEDGEMENTS

Niente Pubblicita, Solo Lettere d'Amore
(No Advertising, Just Love Letters)

My mum, who had high hopes for a peaceful retirement writing her long-awaited romance novel, and instead found herself once again acting as my unofficial recipe tester and copy editor.

Saint Lorenzo, or as he is better known, Lorenzo Putzolu, the most patient man I know, and the very best, too. Long may you dress in six layers in June, and long may we revel in each other's eccentricities. Your passion for history and your hunger have kept me excited about this book even when the chips were so far down they were *sotterraneo*. You washed dishes and grilled aubergines and kept up morale the whole way through. To borrow the words of Jim Broadbent: I just don't work without you.

Mauro and Monica Putzolu, for their support, food, love, advice, encouragement and knowledge. Mauro for his stories and his love for *campagna*, Monica for her generosity and her brusque and brilliant efficiency, and to both for their spirit of fun and discovery.

Zio Mario, for his figs, his zucchini and his stories.

Luigi Manias, for honey and help and his brilliant, bee-keeping, 100-year-old aunt Vera who restores all faith in life.

Holly Peters for good company and help.

Charlotte Bland for always going that little bit further, waking up that little bit earlier and suffering a few more mosquitoes and heatwaves to get the very best shots. May you always be blessed with plenty of figs and fennel.

Allegra Pomilio for her recipe for strawberries marinated with citrus blossoms.

Emily Preece-Morrison for whittling down what was an entire years' worth of rambling and kitchen clutter into the sleek and gleaming beast you now hold in your hands.

Kajal Mistry for being a faithful and committed editor and believing in the project from the outset, and allowing for my slowness.

Tamara Vos for jumping in and saving the day with her beautiful styling and cooking.

Daniel New for his brilliant design and seemingly endless patience.

And finally to our boy, James Amedeo, 'Santino', for making me feel thoroughly ill throughout most of the making/cooking of this book, but then appearing and with one toothless grin making everything else seem irrelevant. I love you more than you will probably ever know.

Published in 2024 by Hardie Grant Books,
an imprint of Hardie Grant Publishing

Hardie Grant Books (London)
5th & 6th Floors
52–54 Southwark Street
London SE1 1UN

Hardie Grant Books (Melbourne)
Building 1, 658 Church Street
Richmond, Victoria 3121

hardiegrantbooks.com

British Library Cataloguing-in-Publication Data.
A catalogue record for this book is available from the British Library.

Wild Figs and Fennel
ISBN: 978-178488-618-9

10 9 8 7 6 5 4 3 2 1

Publishing Director: Kajal Mistry
Project Editor: Emily Preece-Morrison
Design and Illustrations: Daniel New
Photographer: Charlotte Bland
Food Stylists: Letitia Clark and Tamara Vos
Prop Stylists: Letitia Clark and Charlotte Bland
Proofreader: Kathy Steer
Indexer: Hilary Bird
Production Controller: Gary Hayes

Colour reproduction by p2d
Printed and bound in in China by Leo Paper Products Ltd.

Cook's Notes

All butter is unsalted, unless specified otherwise.

All sugar is white granulated, unless
specified otherwise.

Oven temperatures are for fan ovens.

1 teaspoon = 5 ml

1 tablespoon = 15 ml